ANN DREW JACKSON

By
Joan Clark

Illustrations by
Nathan Clark

APC

P.O. Box 23173
Shawnee Mission, Kansas 66283-0173
www.asperger.net

APC

© 2007 Autism Asperger Publishing Co.
P.O. Box 23173
Shawnee Mission, Kansas 66283-0173
www.asperger.net

Publisher's Cataloging-in-Publication

Clark, Joan.
 Ann Drew Jackson / by Joan Clark. -- 1st ed. -- Shawnee Mission, Kan. : Autism Asperger Pub. Co., 2007.

  p. ; cm.

  ISBN-13: 978-1-931282-45-1
  ISBN-10: 1-931282-45-5
  LCCN: 2007922527
  Audience: grades 4-8.

  1. Asperger's syndrome in children--Juvenile fiction. 2. Social acceptance in children--Juvenile fiction. I. Title.

PS3603.L374 A56 2007
813.6--dc22   0703

Cover art and illustrations by Nathan Drew Clark.

Printed in the United States of America.

Dedication

Dedicated To

My husband Ken, children Nathan and Lisa ... and the rest of my family –
   their love keeps me grounded so that I may flourish.

My fellow teachers and staff members –
   their stories of everyday school life give me a foundation for my writing.

My students –
   they have inspired my imagination in a most powerful way.

Prologue

Mid-March, in an Elementary School in Illinois

I wonder what's going to happen to Jackson. He's my friend ... well, he was my friend, until he moved away last week. He was definitely a one-of-a-kind, which I mean in a good way. During his last week of school, I found out something about him, just by accident. Jackson has Asperger Syndrome. It's not a disease or anything. It just describes the way he is, which is a little "different."

I can almost see him on his first day at his new school. He'll be a nervous wreck, bee-lining it down the hallway with his eyes on the floor. He might even run into a kid or two. Who knows what'll happen when he gets in class, but I can guarantee, somebody will notice him before the day is out. First thing he'll do is get his pencils ready, lining them up on his desk according to length, and sharpening the ones that need it. After that, he may grab a couple of 'em, hold one above the other, and flick them back and forth so they make a sort of helicopter. If anyone wants to borrow a pencil, he'll tell them which one they can have and that they have to sharpen it before they give it back to him. No doubt, he'll make a strange comment or two, or maybe even an insulting one. I remember one time when he asked our substitute teacher what that big brown blotch on her face was. It was a birth mark. It seems obvious that you don't ask questions like that right to people's faces, but Jackson did, and that was worth an office referral. In any case, it will be almost hard NOT to notice him.

He might have trouble making friends because, well, that's something he's just not very good at. He never was, but it wasn't like he didn't try. One time he even gave this kid a dollar to be his friend. It was a disaster. The guy and his buddies turned Jackson into the biggest joke ever and made so much fun of him. It was really mean what they did. I should have done something, but I have trouble taking on people like that. Maybe the kids in his new school won't be mean or anything. If they are, he'll need a good, strong friend, NOT a scaredy cat like me – one that can stand up to bullies.

The truth is, Jackson is sort of interesting. He's super smart in some ways and would probably be a very loyal friend. He's funny sometimes, too, and more honest than anybody I've ever known. But most kids don't know that. They ignore him and judge him and mock him. I know how that is because I stutter sometimes, and I get the same treatment. If people don't like how I talk, they don't give me a fair chance. It's sort of like that for Jackson, too. Kids just have to accept him like he is, which sounds easy, but it's not. It took me a long time to figure that out, too long. I feel bad about that, but at least I figured it out. Some kids in my class never did.

I don't know why this is on my mind. I mean, Jackson's pretty much out of my life now. Still, I hope there's someone in his new school that will be his friend. A kind, patient, caring person. That's what he needs.

– Tyler Carson

Chapter One
Partners
Mid-March, in an Elementary School in Washington State

"Okay class, let's partner up," Mrs. Price said, pulling her can of popsicle sticks off her desk. Mrs. Price is my teacher, and she don't like me. She says I got an attitude problem. Well, I s'pose I do. Here we are in the fifth grade, and she's usin' popsicle sticks to decide how we're gonna "partner up," as she likes to say. Please!

"You're going to work in groups of two. Each pair will do a report on an animal of their choice," she explained. Too bad we gotta do her stupid popsicle-stick method to get our partners. It's her way of making sure we get an opportunity to work with all our peers.

She likes the word "peers." Maybe Mrs. Price just likes "P" words. After all, she did marry into a "P" name. And I know she likes to say words like "peers" and "partners." She likes us to do "projects" and work in "pairs," and she loves her "popsicle-stick" method. Oh yeah, and she wants us all to be "perfect" like Pamela (the rich, cute, snotty type) and "polite" like Paul (Mr. Straight A's). That's how we can have a "pleasant" classroom. Maybe me and my partner should choose to do our project on "porcupines" or "penguins" so we can get a "perfect" grade, which, if Mrs. Price had her way, would probably be a "P." (I crack myself up sometimes.)

As for me, I like "S" words, like "sassy," "sarcastic" and "smart aleck." Grownups say I'm "spunky" and "strong-willed," which are code words for "stubborn." And I'm pretty "slick" too, great at weaseling myself out of bad situations. A regular "spitfire," that's me. I even look like "S" words. I'm "skinny" and "scrawny" for my age – 4 feet, 9 inches and 67 pounds. And I have "stupid" hair – red and frizzy and curly and wild. My mom is "single," which is better than being married. She tried that a few times and that was "SORRY!" My grades this year are "sad," which my teacher and mom and counselor say is a real "shame" because I'm so "smart." So as you can see, "S" words work for me and my "screwed-up" life.

About the popsicle-stick method, Mrs. Price has our names on twenty-five popsicle sticks, one for each student in our class. When she wants us to form groups of two, she picks out twelve of the sticks. If you're in that first group, you get to draw a name from the next set of thirteen, and that's your partner. The leftover person gets to pick who to work with. That makes one group of three. Everyone wants to be in that group – less work for the same grade is what I figure. I wanted to work with Paul, Mr. Straight A's, this time, 'cause my science grade stinks. I'm failing, or close to it. Paul wouldn't do nothin' less than perfect, so that would mean I could get an easy A, the best kind to get.

I wasn't in the first group of twelve, but Paul was, and he picked out

Michael. Michael's okay. He's rich, but he don't bother me like some of the other rich kids in my class do. He ain't snotty or nothin' like that. I was feeling good when no one picked my name, 'cause it meant I could pick Michael and Paul to be my partners. That's when Mrs. Price dropped the bombshell.

"Hillary Branson, aren't you lucky to have the leftover popsicle stick!" she said to me, smiling.

"Yeah, I wanna work with Paul and Michael. That's my definite choice," I answered, thinking that for once in our lives we was on the same page.

"No, no, you don't understand," she said. "Tomorrow we are getting a new student in our class. He's moving here from all the way across the country, from Illinois, I think. You get to be the first one to work with him."

Was she for real? Why would I want to work with a new, rich, snotty student? That's the main kind of kid there is in this school. The only reason I'm here is 'cause my mom said my old school was bad, which it was. So last October we moved into this apartment with my grandmother, who is now in the hospital because of a stroke. My mom is either working or visiting my grandma, and I hate it. Nobody else in my class lives in an apartment building, at least not in mine. It's embarrassing – especially 'cause they prob'ly all live in fancy houses. I been invited to a few of them, and they was way ahead of my grandma's place.

"Actually, Mrs. Price," I said, not afraid to challenge her, "my science grade is poor and I'd rather choose my partners. Perhaps someone else would like to work with the new student?" I used good English and tried to look concerned and sincere, but it didn't work.

"No, Hillary, that is not a possibility. You WILL work with the new student, and I expect a good report from both of you." I let out a big sigh and gave her my most scornful look, but that was the end of it. Arguin' don't work with Mrs. Price.

I went home that night to my usual empty apartment. Mom works

the swing shift, which means she leaves the house at noon to go see my
grandma, who's been in "rehab" for I don't know how long. Then she
goes to work at three o'clock and gets off at eleven. She's usually home
by eleven thirty, if she catches the 11:05 city bus. I get phone calls from
her a few times every evening. She says we can afford a phone 'cause
Grandma pays the rent. I'm pretty lonely sometimes. There ain't nobody
in my class I can talk to. Nobody. My mom wants to send me to day care,
but she can't afford it, and so far as I'm concerned, I'm getting too old
anyway. I just turned eleven last month.

Since there wasn't really nothin' to do, I started imagining about
this new kid I got paired up with. Maybe he ain't that rich. Maybe he's
movin' here 'cause he's got a screwed-up life and went to a bad school,
like me. Ha! NO WAY! No one could have it that bad. I do NOT fit in my
school. Oh sure, I can make friends if I want, but I wouldn't be telling
them about my mom's boyfriends or having the electricity turned off last
winter or having to get Christmas presents from churches 'cause we can't
afford nothin'. Kids in my old school knew how that felt, but not in this
one.

Maybe I can get this new kid to do all the work, or at least most of
it. I like drawing pictures for school projects, so that's what I'll do. I got
lots of time – that's for sure. Our TV don't work that good, and we ain't
got no computer, so I gotta think of something to do at night. I'm gettin' good at drawing, 'cause that's all I do. That, and read, but not school
books too much. Just the ones I get at the library.

"B-rrring, b-rrring, b-rrring!" It was 6:45, and Mom was calling
for the second time. She usually called as soon as I got home, early evening, and then 9:15, when she thought I should be going to bed.

"Hi, Hill," she said. "How'd your Monday go today?"

"Fine. I'm workin' on homework right now," I said, knowing
that's what she wanted to hear.

"Do you have a lot?" she asked.

"No," I said, and then pressured her a little about the TV. "I wish you could get the TV fixed. It gets boring here at night sometimes, and it's too quiet."

"I promise, the TV's on my list of important things to do. Next paycheck is already taken up. I gotta get some groceries and you need some new shoes. And I think I can pay off the car. Then it'll be better." Mom was in a wreck a few weeks ago and had to finish paying for the repairs 'fore she could get it back.

"Okay," I said. I knew our situation, so I dropped it.

"So tell me more about your school day," Mom said.

"Well, I'm gonna meet a new kid tomorrow. He'll be my partner on my science project."

"That sounds nice. Did Mrs. Price use that popsicle-stick method you love so much?" Mom teased. She knew how I felt about it.

"Yep," I said. "I was the leftover stick this time, which is how I ended up with this kid."

"Well, I hope he's nice."

"Yeah, me too."

"What do you know about him?"

"He's moving here from Illinois, or some place like that, but that's all."

"That's interesting. Maybe you can kind of help him. You know, the way Pamela did you when you first arrived."

"Yeah," I said, rolling my eyes. If she only knew the way Pamela turned on me, making fun of my hair and my clothes, and just being plain mean. We talked for a few more minutes and then hung up.

I sat in our silent apartment. Alone. I thought about the new kid and wished it was a girl, but oh well. Nothin' ever goes my way, so why would this?

Chapter Two

The New Kid

It's really hard to be-lieve, so let me start from the beginning.

Me and Jenny was walking down the hall, a little slow, talking about Pamela, our favor-ite snotty person to talk about, when bang – some-one barged right through us. It was a boy with a monkey backpack. It looked like something he might have got at the zoo. He was bigger than me, but between the way he barged through us and the look of his backpack, I figured he had to be younger.

"Excuse me," he says, eyes on the floor, after he had already bumped us both apart.

"Jackson, STOP!" a woman's voice yelled behind us. The boy turned around and spoke loud, too loud, like he didn't even notice me and Jenny just a few feet away.

"Room fifteen. The lady said room fifteen. She said it's three doors past the drinking fountain on the right-hand side. The first bell rings in ... ," he pulled back his sleeve and looked at his watch, "approximately one minute and thirty seconds. I have to get to class." Then he turned before the woman could catch up to him, continued looking at the floor, and speed-walked toward room fifteen.

Our room. He was the new kid from Illinois!

Jenny started laughing.

"Dang!" I said, "I ain't workin' with him. Mrs. Price ain't gonna force Mr. Monkey Backpack on me."

"Yeah, I bet," Jenny said, still laughing. She and I both knew that I was stuck with the new kid. Jackson.

Jackson the Joke. I had already decided his nickname.

"Excuse me, girls," the woman said. I assumed it was Jackson's mother. "I couldn't help but hear you."

"We're sorry m'am," said Jenny. "We were just a bit surprised when Jackson barged through us and didn't know what to think." Jenny knew how to be polite a lot better than me.

"Thank you for apologizing, and I'm sorry Jackson barged in between you." Wow, I thought, he must be spoiled rotten. My mom would never apologize for my behavior. Especially for something like that. I'd be the one saying sorry, and would be in big trouble, too.

We followed the woman down the hall and into our room. The

new kid was at his desk, which was beside Mrs. Price's desk. The woman went over to join them. While she and Mrs. Price talked, Jackson fiddled with his fingers and watched his hands. After a few minutes, he pulled out a box of pencils, walked to the back corner of the room, looked around, and then called across the room.

"Excuse me, please, Mrs. Price. I need to sharpen my pencils and the pencil sharpener is not here."

"Jackson," said Mrs. Price, "I'm talking to your mother. You'll have to wait."

"How long do I have to wait? I always like to have my pencils ready before class, and the second bell in my old school rang at eight twenty. That's when we had to be ready. If it rings at eight twenty in this school, I only have seven minutes. I need seven minutes or more to get my pencils ready. Mom will wait while you tell me where the pencil sharpener is, if you ask her nicely. That's why I said 'excuse me, please,' when I asked you. Because that's nice. And I could see you were talking to my mother, so you didn't have to tell me that. I just can't see the pencil sharpener. That's what I need to know."

Geez Lou-eez! Could you believe this kid? Me and Jenny looked at each other and started cracking up. A rumbling of laughter arose all around us. Jackson's mom shrugged at Mrs. Price, quietly said a few words, sort of nodded to her, and then left the room.

That's when Mrs. Price let down the boom, but not on Jackson, who had just talked back to her in front of his mother and the whole class. It was the rest of us she was mad at. She sure could be puzzling some-times – another "P" word for Mrs. Price. After she got us quiet and direct-ed us to do our "daily edit" on the chalkboard, she told Jackson where the pencil sharpener was. He took at least five minutes sharpening a bunch of pencils, and another wad of time lining them up along the top edge of his desk. He was bizarre. That's my grandma's word for weird. And he was my science partner. I wanted to die.

Finally, after Jackson was all finished with his pencils came the introduction.

"Class, this is Jackson Thomas. He's moved here from Illinois, which is quite a long way. Who would like to ask Jackson some questions about himself?"

Nobody raised their hand. We just looked around at each other like, "What in the world would you ask him?" That's not how it was when I joined the class back in October. Everyone had all these questions. Too many questions. That's what I remember – too many.

"Well then," Mrs. Price said, reaching for her popsicle stick can. "I guess I'll have to draw a name." And as my rotten luck would have it, of course, she drew mine. I thought about his first-grade monkey backpack, which was hanging from his chair, and his pencil problem, but I didn't know how to turn those into questions that wouldn't get me in trouble.

"Hmmm, well, hmmm, um, how far is Illinois from here?" I finally asked, totally not caring about the answer.

"Approximately two thousand two point seven miles, according to my dad's odometer," Jackson replied. That was precise, for sure, I thought. Mrs. Price probably liked the preciseness, being that it was another "P" word.

Pamela was the next name out of the popsicle-stick can. Here's the thing about Pamela – she gets away with everything. She's got Mrs. Price totally fooled. So when she said, "Gee, Jackson, I really love your backpack. Where did you get it?" I knew she was making fun of him, but Mrs. Price didn't.

"I agree, Pamela. That is an interesting backpack. I'll bet he got it at an interesting place." Gag me.

"I got it at my house," said Jackson. I snickered a little. It was a good comeback to Mrs. Price's "interesting place" comment.

"What do you mean by that?" asked Mrs. Price.

"I mean, I got it at my house. In the kitchen."

"I'm still a little confused," continued Mrs. Price. "Is that where you keep it?"

"No, that's where my mom gave it to me," Jackson said.

"Well, where did your mom get it?" asked Mrs. Price.

"Probably my room. That's where I keep it."

"Well then who bought it for you?" Mrs. Price was bound and determined to get to the bottom of this.

"I think my grandma."

"Well then, your mom must have gotten it from your grandma to give to you," Mrs. Price explained.

"Mom didn't tell me where she got it, but Grandma's name was on the card. That's how I know she got it for me."

"What card?" asked Mrs. Price.

"My birthday card," answered Jackson.

"So you got the backpack as a birthday present from your grandma?" Mrs. Price asked.

"Yes, that's exactly right."

"Well, that's what Pamela was trying to find out all along. Right, Pam?"

"Right. I was really hoping I could find one like it," she answered pleasantly. Liar. I'd bet five bucks on her makin' fun of Jackson and his backpack once Mrs. Price was gone.

"I'll call my grandma and find out where she got it," said Jackson. "She might have gotten it at the San Diego Zoo, since she lives in San Diego. It's approximately one thousand two hundred and sixty miles from here to San Diego, so that's four hundred twenty miles a day for three days. That's a long way to go for a backpack."

"Thank you so much, Jackson," Pamela said, in her syrupy sweet voice. Wait until he finds out how mean she can be. She's so dang sneaky, too, that the teacher never finds out.

The questions went on for a few more minutes, along with the odd answers. Jackson seemed to be nervous. He fiddled with his pencils and wouldn't look at nobody.

Great, I thought, just great. What kind of partner is he going to be? I was hoping for someone smart who could take over the whole project, like Paul would have done. Instead, I got this partner that don't even understand how to answer simple questions.

Jackson the Joke, that's just my luck.

Chapter Three

The Science Project

It was lunchtime at last. Tuesday lunch was pizza, my favorite. I sat by Jenny. She's my best friend these days, and we had a lot to talk about, including Jackson. But Mrs. White, the lunchroom lady, who I usually like, messed it up. Jackson was sitting by hisself three seats away from us, at the very end of the

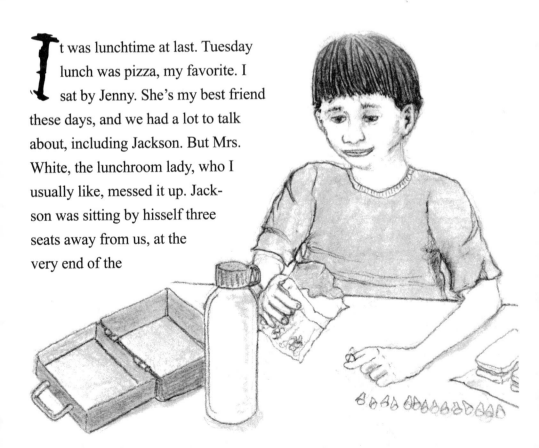

table, and she must not have liked that. She's real nice, but she ain't got no sense sometimes.

"Oh, you must be the new boy from Illinois," she said in her friendly way. "We can't have you sitting all by yourself."

"Well, I was from Illinois, but now I'm from Washington because that's where we moved," he answered.

"Well, aren't you a clever little jokester," Mrs. White answered. She gave Jackson a pat on the back, and he sort of jumped.

"Sorry child, I didn't mean to surprise you."

"My name is Jackson. Jackson Evan Thomas. My initials are J-E-T, and they spell jet. Most people call me Jackson, but if you can't remember my name, you can call me 'child.'"

"You are so funny! I think people are going to really like you. You shouldn't be sitting by yourself. You need to have other people enjoyin' your company. Why don't you join Hillary and Jenny here?"

So Jackson sat across from me and Jenny. He didn't look at us. He didn't say "hi" to us. He just placed his blue plastic lunchbox on the table-top, undid the latch, and opened it up. I thought the contents must have been interesting as long as he stared at them. But they wasn't nothin' special.

A sandwich, no crust, a thermos of something, a banana, and a bag of these little cone-shaped salty snacks, sort of like chips or crackers. I'd seen them before, but didn't know their name. He pulled out each item, one at a time, and lined them up from left to right in front of him. Then he counted his cone-shaped snacks.

"Twenty-five," I heard him say under his breath, "twenty-five tor-nadoes."

Hmm, I thought, so that's what they're called. Then I turned to Jenny, who was studying Jackson, too.

"Think he's actually going to talk to us?" I asked quietly.

"I don't know," she said, "but if he does, why don't you try to be nice to him?" She might be the only friend I ever had that could tell me things like that without making me blow up.

"You mean I can't say nothin' 'bout his backpack or his pencil problem or his mommy watching after him?" I asked, smiling, just to see what she'd do.

"You are so bad. I don't know why I'm even friends with you sometimes," Jenny protested, but there was a tinge of a smile behind her eyes. I knew she wasn't mad.

"Well, I guess you could go hang around with Pamela," I shot back. A great comeback, as rotten as Pamela was to Jenny.

"Yeah, well, I'm going to have to, because she's my science partner." She rolled her eyes and sighed.

"No way!" I said. Poor Jenny. I thought I had it bad with Monkey Backpack Boy here, but at least he seemed harmless enough. Pamela could be heartless, just really mean, if you wasn't in the right crowd. People sometimes think I'm mean, but I ain't, if you really know me. I just got to protect myself, and the only thing I've figured out that works is attitude. Bad attitude. And tough, too.

"So, Jackson," Jenny began, "did you know that you and Hillary are working on a science project together?" Jackson sort of looked at her, but not really, and scrunched his eyebrows.

"No, we're not," he said.

"Yes, we are," I answered.

"I don't know Hillary," he said. He must have been distracted by my frizzy hair, 'cause he didn't look at me; just my hair.

"You're talking to her," Jenny said, pointing at me.

"Oh." He picked up a tornado snack and rolled it in his fingers. Then he spoke to Jenny, very matter-of-factly, "I didn't know her name. I was talking to her and now I'm talking to you. But I'm not doing a science project with her."

"Well I'm talkin' to you," I shot back at him. "And Jenny's right. She always tells the truth and we ARE working on a science project together."

"No, we're not," Jackson said again.

"Yes, we are. We are working together," I insisted.

"No, we're not," Jackson repeated.

"Yes, we are," I said. Jenny's head bobbed back and forth between us as she watched the argument go nowhere. Finally, I decided to change my way of arguing.

"Jackson, ask Mrs. Price. She'll tell you. We really are working on a science project."

"No, we're not," he said to my hair, which is where he was still looking.

"How do you know?" I asked, trying hard to make my new method work. I was going to blow up if this argument went any further.

"Because we're eating lunch," he said. "Is eating lunch a science project in Washington? It isn't in Illinois."

It took me a second to get what he was saying, but I have to admit, he really got us. He set us up with all his serious looks and "no we're nots" and then came in for the kill. The joke was on us, totally. Me and Jenny looked at each other, and then busted up. Jackson finally started laughing, too, but only after keeping a slight frown going for a while. My stomach hurt from laughing by the time Jenny finally spoke up.

"I wish eating lunch was a science project," she said. Then she cracked up again.

"It could be," Jackson said, returning to his serious look while twisting his tornado snack in his fingers. He stared at his fingers as he sort of mumbled on. "You see this little snack. Well, it represents a tornado. Did you know there are five levels of tornadoes? F-1, F-2, F-3, F-4, and F-5. Dr. Fujita developed the tornado scale in 1971. Each category is determined by wind speed. An F-5 tornado has wind speeds of 261 to 318 miles per hour. It causes incredible damage and is the most dangerous of all. An F-4 has wind speeds of 207 to 260 miles per hour. It also causes damage, but ..."

Me and Jenny stopped laughing. We looked at him, looked at each other, and then we shook our heads. Who was this kid? Finally, I interrupted.

"Hey, Jackson, can I eat one of those tornado snacks?" I asked.

"Then I'll only have twenty-four to eat. My mom always gives me tornado snacks in multiples of five. On Dr. Fujita's scale, there are five levels of tornadoes, so I like my tornadoes to come in multiples of five. I could give you each five, and then I would have fifteen, which is a multiple of five. That would be okay with me."

"Okay," I said, thinking how strange he was. One thing's for sure, I'm glad our science project was on animals and not weather. He just seemed a little too intense on this whole tornado thing.

He gave us the snacks one at a time, talking about tornadoes, wind speeds, Dr. Fujita, and I don't know what else. Me and Jenny ignored him and talked between ourselves. I had a feeling that working on a science project with him was going to be an experience like I never had before.

And not a good one.

Chapter Four

The Definition of "Healthy"

"**Y**eah, and then guess what he done," I said to my mom. We was having our usual after-school phone conversation, and I had to tell her about Jackson. I did NOT want to be his partner, not after what he done to Jenny.

"What?" asked Mom. She didn't have long to talk, so I couldn't go into too much detail.

"Well, Mrs. Price asked him who he made friends with. You know, the same way she asked me about that on my first day of school. He said me and Jenny."

"That's nice," Mom said.

"Not really," I corrected her, "'cause then he talked about my frizzy hair and how hoom-dee, or something like that, makes it frizzy. But it ain't really frizzy, he says. It's just very soft, and he likes soft. He even tried to touch it, but I pulled away. Ain't that weird?"

"I think you mean humidity and yeah, it is kinda weird."

"He thought it was a compliment. Mrs. Price asked him to say something nice about me, and that's what he said. He ain't right. I don't wanna do my science project with him."

"Just give him a chance," Mom answered.

"But wait, you ain't even heard the worst of it," I continued. She just had to hear what Jackson did to Jenny. It was plain wrong, and I didn't want to be partners with him. Period, the end.

When Jackson told Mrs. Price that me and Jenny was his friends, she asked us to say something nice about him. So we said how much he knows about tornadoes and how he shared his tornado snacks with us. Then she asked him to tell something nice about us. She did that to me when I was new to the class, so I knew the whole routine. Anyways, that's how I got my frizzy hair compliment from Jackson (if that's what you want to call it).

Then he had to say something about Jenny. So he stared at her for a while with a crinkled, serious face. Suddenly he smiled and thrust his hand up high with his finger pointing to the ceiling.

"I know!" he said. "She's a healthy girl. I think she's very healthy."

"Healthy?" Mrs. Price responded.

"Yes, she's very healthy," he said, still smiling. "'Healthy' is a nice word."

"I suppose she is," Mrs. Price commented. I didn't get how that was a compliment. I think a lot of us didn't ,'cause we was lookin' at each other and shakin' our heads, like we was confused. Someone whispered, "Why the heck is that a compliment?" Mrs. Price musta thought the same thing, 'cause of what she said.

"Actually, lots of people in our class are healthy, Jackson. In fact, I think all of us are."

"I don't think so," said Jackson, "but even if we are, we aren't very, very, very healthy."

"Wow! You really think Jenny is healthy," said Mrs. Price, and then she turned to Jenny and smiled. "Isn't that nice?" Jenny smiled and nodded her head. That's when Pamela stepped in with her great big bragging mouth.

"Excuse me, Mrs. Price, but I just want you to know that I am the top cheerleader in our squad at the gym where I go, and I won first place in the mile run last week in P.E. class. I think I am at least as healthy as Jenny."

"No you're not," Jackson piped in right away. I laughed to myself.

"It's hard to know how healthy people are," said Mrs. Price.

"Well, she's not as healthy as Jenny," Jackson mumbled, and he sort of looked down. Pamela shook her head, scowled at him, and blew out a bunch of air. That's when I got my idea. I spoke in my snottiest "Pamela" voice, barely loud enough for her to hear.

"Excuse me, Mrs. Price, I just want you to know that I am the top soccer player on my soccer team, and I think I'm at least as healthy as Pamela." It was a lie. But I sounded just like her, and the kids that heard me giggled.

"That's funny, you sure can't run too well for a soccer player. Was that last place you got – or next to the last – in the mile run?" Pamela snapped back quietly. I could hear some oooo's. She got me back. Me and Jenny had walked that mile run that she won, 'cause we decided to be last on purpose. But I know I could beat Pamela if I wanted to. Jackson over-heard her. His head popped up from his finger-staring, and he spoke loud enough for everyone to hear.

"Maybe Hillary can't run too well because she's not healthy." What a jerk! Who did he think he was, ganging up with Pamela on me. I was really mad.

"I can beat everyone in this class in a race if I want to, and I AM healthy!" I yelled, a little out of control.

"Hillary, STOP now!" Mrs. Price said firmly. Then she turned to Jackson. "It wasn't nice of you to say that about Hillary. You've probably never seen her run, and how would you know about her health?"

"She's not healthy because she's skinny," Jackson said. "'Healthy' is a nice word for fat, so fat people are healthy and healthy can't be skinny be-cause skinny is the opposite of fat. But it's not nice to call people fat because it hurts their feelings, so that's why I said Jenny is very, very, very healthy."

Jenny's face fell and her hands came up to her mouth, but Jackson must not have noticed 'cause he kept right on. "That's like analogies I'm doing. I was working on those in my last school. And my mom told me not to call people fat, and she taught me about saying healthy instead of fat. That's why healthy is a compliment. Because it's nice."

Pamela looked at Jenny and giggled a little. So did some other kids, but they was all kind of quiet about it so the teacher wouldn't notice. They'd get Jenny later on. Jenny's face went beet red, and water welled up in her eyes. She was fat, the fattest one in our class, but she was trying to lose weight. Her mom always had her on this or that diet. Everyone made fun of her, except me.

"Jackson, this is unacceptable!" said Mrs. Price. "You need to apologize and then go out in the hall." He wrinkled his forehead, rubbed his hands together and stared at them, but he didn't say anything.

"Jackson, you have five seconds. You hear me?" warned Mrs. Price. He kept staring at his hands and started rocking back and forth a little.

"I think I know," he mumbled, well past the five-second time limit he was given. "I'm sorry I said the definition of healthy. I'm not supposed to do that. I think that's what my mom said. I'm sorry." Then he got up, walked out the door barely into the hallway, turned around, and looked into room.

"All the way out in the hallway," said Mrs. Price. So he took one step back, but kept staring into the room.

"It was awful, Mom," I said, "and when we was dismissed, a bunch of kids kept calling Jenny healthy on the way out to the bus. Finally, she started cryin', the quiet cry that's real sad. Just big tears drippin' down her face. I ain't doin' no project with that boy. I just refuse."

"Mrs. Price knows what Jackson did. If you really have a problem with him, just tell her. She'll understand," Mom said.

"You know she don't like me," I answered. My anger was creeping up. Mom just sighed.

"I'm really busy with Grandma. They're teaching me how to do her therapy so she can come home, and I'm putting in a lot of hours. You know how much we need the money." It was her way of saying she wasn't going to call.

"You never got time for me!" I yelled. "It's Grandma-work-Grandma-work. What about me?"

"I'm trying Hill, I really am."

"So will you call?" I asked, practically begging. Mrs. Price don't listen to nothin' I say. I know it's 'cause I got an attitude and a bad temper. I'm workin' on it with Mrs. Lorrey, my social worker. But this time I had a right to lose my temper and be mad. I felt so sorry for Jenny, and I needed my mom's help or else I'd be stuck with Jackson, the rudest kid ever.

"I just don't have no time to call," Mom finally said. "Besides, you can be his partner. He didn't do nothin' to you. It sounds like the other kids was the ones doin' the real teasing, not Jackson." There was a moment of silence and I felt a big lump forming in my throat. Pamela and her friends and some other kids was the ones teasing Jenny, but they wasn't my partners. Jackson was. I didn't want nothin' to do with anyone that hurt Jenny's feeling so bad.

"Thanks for nothing!" I tried to yell but it barely came out. I slammed down the phone, tried to swallow down the lump, and wiped a tear from my face. Nobody cared, not even my mom.

Chapter Five

"P" Is for Perfect

I pumped myself high, high into the air on the swing in the playground area at our apartment. My eyes were closed and the wind blew through my hair. Mrs. Lorrey had helped me figure out about swinging. It's what I do to calm down. I been doin' it ever since I was little, and now I do it on purpose to help me settle down.

I kept thinking about my mom never havin' no time for me, my grandma bein' so sick, my mom and me bein' so poor, no TV, and nobody ever home but me. I was lonely. Then I changed from feeling sorry about me to school – Jackson sayin' how fat Jenny was, Jenny cryin', and everyone makin' fun of her. And then slowly my mind drifted into what happened earlier in the day when we started on our science project. It was a different kind of Jackson. Actually, it was more like the one I met at lunch, the joking one.

Early in the afternoon, Mrs. Price had explained our science project to us. Each group had to agree on an animal and write a report together. The report had to contain all this information, and we had to show what the animal looked like. After passing out a handout and giving a long explanation, Mrs. Price finally told us to find our science partners. I got up and headed over to Jackson's desk.

"I'm your partner. That's what me and Jenny meant when we was saying I was working on a science project with you," I said.

"Oh," replied Jackson, straightening out his pencils.

"So, do you have an idea for what we should do?" I asked.

"No," Jackson said. "I need to sharpen the fourth pencil."

"Not now you don't. We need to agree on something so we can get started."

"We can do a science report on tornadoes," he suggested. "I know a whole lot about tornadoes."

"What's you talking about?" I asked. Mrs. Price had spent the last twenty minutes telling us about our ANIMAL report.

"I'm talking about tornadoes. You know. Remember there are five levels, and five is the most ..."

"We have to do ANIMALS. Ain't you been listening?" I blurted out.

"Oh, well, sometimes tornadoes have an impact on the habitat of animals, like, for instance ..."

"NO! We're doing animals, NOT tornadoes," I insisted. My face was inches from his and I had my hands on my hips. He looked at my frizzy hair and tried to touch it, but I pulled away. Then he studied his line of pencils on his desk.

"Well, I need to sharpen my fourth pencil," he finally said again. I shook my head as he picked up his pencil and walked to the sharpener. While I watched him, an idea popped into my head. I could play a joke on him, just like he had done to me and Jenny at lunch. He didn't have no idea what Mrs. Price said about our project, so I could say anything I wanted.

"You know we have to do our report on an animal," I said when he came back, and then I started my joke. "But we can't do monkeys." Jackson frowned and scrunched up his face.

"I know a lot about monkeys and tornadoes," he said. "I want to do our report on monkeys or tornadoes."

"Well, we can't," I said, and then added more to my joke. "Wasn't you listenin'? Mrs. Price said she's only givin' perfect grades to people who do animals that begin with P. That's her favorite letter. That's why she don't like me that much. 'Cause my name begins with H. She really likes Pamela and Paul a lot better than everyone else in the class. Their names begin with P."

"Well, my name begins with J. Do you think she likes me?" Jackson asked. He was real serious, pretending like Mrs. Price would actually make a stupid rule like that. I knew he was just jokin' around, like at lunch. I wasn't gonna fall for his tricks again.

"Nah, she don't like you," I said, keeping the joke going. He frowned and shook his head.

"And she don't want us doing no reports on monkeys," I continued. "Sorry, and we can't do nothin' on porcupines or penguins or poodles 'cause some other kids already got them taken up for their project."

Jackson shook his head and looked concerned. "This is going to be hard. I really want to do monkeys. We could do Rhesus monkeys. They're very interesting." He didn't crack a smile and seemed really good at playing along with this joke, except he didn't get the "P" part. So I fixed that.

"Nope. We can't do no Rhesus monkeys. They begin with an R." I turned my head away so he wouldn't see me giggling. "Can't do gorillas or hyenas or none of 'em. Remember, they gotta begin with P to get a perfect grade." Jackson started twiddling his pencils, and then he sighed real loud. He was way better at keeping serious than me.

"Well," he said, "I know something that's not a monkey that begins with a P. Maybe we could do that one."

"It might already be taken," I warned, trying hard to be as serious as him.

"It's a potto," he said.

"Oh, that's taken," I answered, like I knew what a potto was. It was hard to keep a straight face. Just then Mrs. Price walked by.

"Have you decided what you want to do for your report?" she asked.

"I want to do pottos, but someone took pottos," Jackson said.

"What are they?" asked Mrs. Price.

"Pottos are not monkeys, but they do belong to the primate family, like monkeys. But their suborders are different," Jackson said. I just stared at him. That was one weird explanation.

"Oh," said Mrs. Price. "And why do you think someone took them?"

"Hillary said so," he answered.

"Is that right?" she said, and then she turned to me. "And who do you think took the pottos, Hillary?" I shrugged my shoulders and looked down.

"Do you think I need to talk to Mrs. Lorrey about how you're doing with your little problem?" she asked. My "little problem" was lying, according to them. But I don't really lie. Not that much. This time, I was just jokin' around. That ain't no lie.

"No m'am. I was just jokin' around," I said as respectfully as I could.

"Your joking around is not funny, Hillary, not at all," scolded Mrs. Price. Then she turned to Jackson, "You can do a report on pottos if you want. Hillary will have to agree. She's lost the privilege of choosing. You'll choose for both of you."

"Oh, she'll like pottos," he said. "They begin with the letter P, and we want to get a perfect grade." Mrs. Price looked at me with suspicious eyes. I wondered why Jackson was hinting about our joke. It was getting me in trouble.

"I'm sure you'll do well, Jackson. Just make sure that Hillary is doing her fair share." Boy, did that make me mad! I sighed real loud and glared at her.

"But I thought she had to do pottos. She won't like doing fair share," he said. Then he paused, smiled, and pointed his finger up in the air, "unless fair share begins with a ph." Mrs. Price shook her head and let out a sigh.

"I just mean you shouldn't do all the work. Hillary should do the same amount," she said.

"Ohhhhhhhhh," he said, stretching the word out for five seconds or longer, like this was something he hadn't already figured out. Then he added, "Mrs. Price, my uncle calls me Pipsqueak and Pipsqueak begins with the letter P."

"I know," she said, shaking her head again, "but that's not something I would call you. I'll stick with Jackson." She turned and headed to the next group.

What a jerk, I thought. He just carried my P joke way too far. It ain't funny when someone ruins your joke. I should've told him off, but I didn't.

I swung and swung for a long time. The whole Jenny story had really upset me. And even though Jackson might think he's good at jokes, he ain't that great. He practically ruined mine. I had good reasons to be mad at him.

That was when I saw the shock of my life. Around the corner of the far apartment building came three people – Jackson, his mother, and a girl. Actually, she was a teenager. What was they doin' here in these crappy old apartments?

I drug my feet to stop the swing and set out to investigate.

Chapter Six

The Spy

The Seattle Seahawk ball cap lay at the corner of the playground bench, like a gift for me.

I pulled my frizzy hair into a pony-tail, grabbed the ball cap, and scrunched my hair into it. It was a little too big, so the visor covered my face pretty good. In my disguise I took off across the grass.

I was a little worried they might notice me running, but got lucky again. Jackson or his mom, or that girl with them, musta dropped a grocery bag, because they was all bending down picking up stuff. I snuck behind a bush, and they never saw me. My plan was to follow them and listen to what they had to say, kind of like a spy. I was gonna pretend like I was listenin' to music. My left index finger would be holdin' a speaker to my ear, and my right hand would be under my sweatshirt by my waistband, like I was holdin' a CD player. I could bounce around quietly behind them. If they saw me, they'd think I was listenin' to music and wouldn't talk to me.

That's what I hoped. After school, I had changed from my pink skirt and white sweater to a pair of old jeans and a sweatshirt. Between that and the ball cap to hide my hair and face, there wasn't no way that Jackson would recognize me.

"I can't believe you didn't see that crack? You need to watch where you're going," the girl said as they was picking up the final items. She had to be his sister. They sort of looked alike, 'cept she was taller and had long hair.

"I watched in front of me, not down by my feet," he said.

"Well duh," she joked.

"I was practicing," Jackson said. "Today a girl in my class asked if I could see the craters Jenny made in the floor from walking and I told her I didn't see any. Then she told me to keep looking down, 'cause Jenny made craters a lot. I told her I would and kept looking down, and then she laughed, so I think she was making a joke. So I laughed, too."

"And so what's your point?" asked the girl. I was glad she said that, 'cause I didn't have no idea what he meant.

"And so I had to look down for craters, and I had already looked down all day because it's a new school and I like the circles in the square tiles on the floor and I know I'm not always supposed to look down because it's not friendly so I was practicing looking up because we've been at these apartments five days so I know this place better than the new school."

"Jackson," his mother interrupted, "people don't make craters in the floor when they walk."

"Well, that girl in my class said that Jenny made craters," Jackson said, defending himself.

This conversation was too weird. I wanted to hear the rest of it, but they started walkin' down the sidewalk with the mom carrying the bag of stuff. I came out from the bush, one hand by my ear, the other under my sweatshirt, kind of bouncing to the beat of pretend music.

"She was making fun of you, idiot, and she was making even more fun of Jenny," said his sister.

"Mom, Liz called me idiot and I'm not an idiot."

"Stop it, Liz," Jackson's mom said. Then she turned her head toward Jackson, but he didn't turn toward her – his head just kept facing straight forward. "Jackson," she said, "I have a feeling that girl wasn't being nice."

"Oh no, Mom, she's very nice. She likes my monkey backpack and might drive one thousand two hundred and sixty miles to the San Diego Zoo to get one. That's a long way." His mom shook her head and sighed.

"Just remember, some people seem nice, but they're really not." I was glad his mom said that. It made me think she was already onto Pamela, and they've never even met each other yet.

"But she's nice, and the teacher likes her a lot. That's what Hillary told me." My ears perked up when I heard my name.

"Well, I guess she would know. Isn't she the girl who will be your science partner?"

"Yeah. She has frizzy hair, but it's not frizzy; it's just soft. The humidity makes it seem that way. That' because ..."

"Stop!" Liz said. "Don't be boooooorrrring, which is what you're going to be if you start explaining about humidity again for the ka-jillionth time." She really sounded bossy, but I guess he didn't notice, 'cause his answer was so nice.

"Oh, okay," he replied, like his sister had just been polite. "I'll just explain it to Mom later. That's what we worked out. Right, Mom?"

"Right," his mom said, adding, "Jackson, we're going to change your schedule a little bit today when we get in the apartment."

"But I get to watch the Weather Channel at six thirty right after dinner."

"That's right. But we need to add in a discussion time."

"That will be a good time for me to tell you about humidity."

"That's not discussing, Jackson. Remember, we talked about that? That's more like lecturing, because you know a whole lot more about weather than I do."

"When will you let me lecture to you about weather?" Jackson went on.

"Later tonight, after you're done watching TV. I'll write it on the schedule." She paused for a second and added, "The discussion we need to have is not about weather, and we won't be allowed to mention weather. It's going to be about commenting on people's appearance."

"I had to comment on people today. The teacher made me give two girls compliments."

"I know. That's why we need to talk."

"'Cause I got in trouble? 'Cause I said Jenny was healthy and then accidentally told the meaning?" Jackson asked.

"Oh man!" said Liz, who was walking ahead of them. Then she spun around to face him and noticed me. I kept bouncing and moving from side to side with my eyes sort of closed. Please, I thought, please think I'm into my "music."

Luckily, she did. At least that's what I thought.

"Don't tell me you told her she was healthy and then explained to everyone that meant fat. That's bad! That's really mean," his sister blurted.

"It is not mean. I was giving her a compliment, and healthy is a nice way to say fat, and I was trying to be nice. Right, Mom?" Jackson went on.

"We are going to put a discussion time in your schedule when we get inside. That's when we'll talk about it. Not now."

A discussion time? Why in the world do they have to schedule a discussion time, I wondered.

"Okay," said Jackson. "It's now four twenty-eight. I have seventeen minutes to get changed. Then I have to start my homework and work on it for thirty minutes. Then I'll set the table and make sure my pencils are okay to start my homework again. Then I'll do more homework. I'm researching pottos, so I have to use the computer, and I have some books, too."

"Jackson," his Mom said, "Liz will set the table tonight and make sure your pencils are sharpened properly. That's the part of the schedule we'll change. We'll make that our discussion time." Liz let out a loud moan. I smiled, 'cause I could picture me doin' the same thing.

They was coming to a stop at an apartment on the opposite side of the compound from mine. I danced right past them, since it would be stupid for me to stand there. I kept wondering why they had to schedule a discussion time. What was that about?

"Hey you! You in the Seattle Seahawks ball cap!" I heard Jackson's sister yell once I got past them. "You've been spying on us? That's not too friendly."

I kept dancin' away like I didn't hear her. She was right on both counts. I was spying, and I wasn't bein' friendly. That's 'cause I didn't wanna talk to no one that treated Jenny like Jackson did. Once I was around the corner, I ran around the back of the building and all away around the apartment complex until I got to the bench where I found the ball cap. I threw it down and ran to my apartment.

Time to change clothes again. I got my wrinkled dirty khakis out of the laundry and a long-sleeved, faded-out blue t-shirt. I threw them on, along with my mom's too-big yellow windbreaker.

Then I ran back out to the swing to think about the conversation I had just overheard. It was kind of fun bein' a spy.

Maybe it was a start of a career for me.

Chapter Seven

Jokes, Lies, and Tempers

"Hillary, you know it's just not true," said Mrs. Lorrey. Wednesday morning started out really bad for me. That's why I was sent to the social worker, and I didn't want to hear what she had to say.

"But it was a joke, not a lie," I insisted. I had calmed down from earlier in the day, but could feel myself getting angry again. "You tellin' me I ain't allowed to tell jokes without bein' called a liar. FINE. I can be like you want me to be and not be my-self." I crossed my arms in front of my chest and clamped my lips shut. I knew that would get to her.

"That's not what I'm saying. It's just that Jackson didn't know it was a joke. He really thinks, thanks to you, that Mrs. Price prefers the letter P. To him, it was a lie." I wanted to roll my eyes, but kept a straight face. I wasn't talking or showing my thoughts. Period. I was mad. I can't do nothin' with-out people calling me a liar. It just wasn't right. A joke ain't a lie. It's a joke.

"You know, you really need to get to know Jackson. There's more to him than meets the eye." She was nuts. I wasn't plannin' on knowing Jackson. What I figured out after one day made me think: WEIRD. I had enough problems without adding "weird" to them. Besides, I still couldn't get past him makin' fun of Jenny. We sat in silence for a minute or so. I could feel Mrs. Lorrey's eyes on me, but I pretended I didn't and refused to say a word. I just wanted to go back to class.

"You know, I have things to do, too, so I'll just get out my work until you're ready to talk," she finally said. I hoped she had a lot of work, 'cause I could sit all day without talking. I can handle being called a liar when I lie. But when I don't, well, it just ain't right.

And it really wasn't right what happened to Jenny this morning. I had to defend her. I laid my head on the table, face down, and thought about how I ended up here in the first place.

O O O

It was before school when the trouble started. Me and Jenny was by the back closet talking when Jackson came up to us. He stood practi-cally between us and stared at our shoes. We looked at him, looked at each other, and stopped talking.

"Excuse me," he finally said, keeping his eyes on the floor. "I'm sorry." Then he turned around to walk away. I grabbed him by his arm before he could leave and whoa – he jumped! It was like I shocked him or something.

"What's you sorry about?" I asked.

"I'm not supposed to say it," he said.

"You ain't supposed to say what you're sorry about? That don't make no sense at all," I snipped back.

"I'm not supposed to say the word any more," he explained.

"That's okay," Jenny said. "I know what you mean."

I touched his arm again as he was turning around to leave 'cause I remembered the talk his mother wanted to have with him, and I had something to say. He jumped and told me not to touch him.

"Okay," I said, "but I wanna know, did your mom tell you to say sorry?"

"Yes," he admitted and started to turn around.

"If you don't want me to touch you no more, then you stay right here 'til I'm done talking to you," I blurted out before he could leave. I had a point I wanted to make. He turned around and looked at me, sort of, so I continued. "Here's what I gotta say: If your mom told you to say sorry, then it ain't worth the paper it's written on." That's one of my grandma's favorite expressions.

"I didn't write it on paper," he said. I gave him the "Well, duh!" look and shook my head.

Then he smiled and spoke, "Is that an idiom? I learned about idioms, like 'green with envy,' which doesn't mean you're green because people really aren't green. It just means ..."

"I don't know if it's an idiom," I said. He was changing the subject, and I didn't like it. He needed to know that apologizing because your mom told you to ain't really apologizing.

"'Green with envy' means you're really jealous," he continued, "and I know more idioms, too, like 'ants in your pants,' which means you can't sit still but you really don't have ants and ..."

"Stop!" I sort of yelled, louder than I wanted to. But he didn't. So I touched him. Actually, I poked him in the chest. He stopped immediately.

"Here's an idiom for you," I said. "'It ain't worth the paper it's written on' means it don't mean nothin'. You don't apologize 'cause your mom told you to. You apologize 'cause you're really sorry. You got it?" My hands was on my hips, my face was right in his face, and my voice was bossy. He WOULD get my point!

"Hillary, just leave him be," Jenny sort of whispered. Actually, Jackson looked a little scared or confused or something.

"Oh," he said. "My mom told me to say sorry, and I really am sorry, so does that mean its not worth the paper it's written on?"

"Never mind. Just get outta here," I said. He walked over to his desk. I watched him as he examined his pencils and took some of them over to the pencil sharpener. He laid all but one of the pencils down by the sharpener and started sharpening the remaining one. It was kind of interesting to watch, but I got interrupted.

"Hey, Hilly, Hilly, Hilly!" Pamela softly called to me as she headed back toward the closet. Then came the zinger. "How's Healthy, Healthy, Healthy doing?" She laughed and so did the kids putting away their backpacks in the closet. Jenny pretended she didn't hear Pamela, but I didn't.

"Ain't you the clever girl, copyin' off yesterday. You ain't got a new idea so you just gotta go and copy." I rolled my eyes and turned around to see what Jen was doing. She shook her head at me and gave me The Look, meaning I was supposed to stay outta it.

"Well, I was just making a little joke, nothing serious," Pamela said. "Honestly, you need to lighten up." Then she tapped Jenny on her back. "Thank heavens you have a sense of humor, Health – I mean Jenny. You need to work on your friend here. No wonder no one likes her." That's when Jenny turned around and spoke up.

"I like her. To me, she's prob'ly the nicest person in this class." That was as much as she could muster. I could tell by her voice she was getting upset. I know that feeling, the big lump in the throat before you blow up or start crying.

"Well, she needs to work on being nice to more people than just you," Pamela said, like I wasn't even there. "She needs to take a joke, just like you, Healthy Girl – you know I don't mean anything bad by that. You're smart enough to take a joke." Jenny sort of smiled and then turned around toward her backpack. Her face was getting red, and her eyes was filled with water. I saw her take a deep, hard gulp. A few kids stood around snickering at her, and that's when I lost it.

I got really mad, out-of-control mad.

Wham! I pushed Pamela to the ground and called her a bad word. Across the room, Mrs. Price's voice shot like thunder and I stopped in my tracks. Which was a good thing, considerin' how mad I was.

Mrs. Price sent me out to the hallway. That meant Pamela would tell her story first and anything I would say would be considered a lie. Pamela and her friends was always lyin' but the teacher didn't know 'cause they made sure they was all tellin' the same story.

○　○　○

"Hillary," Mrs. Lorrey suddenly said. "Let's change the subject." I popped out of my daydream, and tried to remember what subject we had been on.

"Let's talk again about how you got here this morning." I retold the story, and then remembered I was mad and wasn't s'posed to talk. Oh well, it was okay. Mrs. Lorrey was always doing that to me. Getting me mad so I would never talk to her again, and then making me forget about it so I did talk.

"I'll tell you what. I know why you're mad at Pamela, I really do. But I'm still unclear about Jackson," she said.

"Well, duh! He started the whole thing with his 'healthy' comment. I gotta do my science project with him, but that's it." I crossed my arms across my chest. That meant I wasn't changin' my mind.

"He really wasn't trying to be hurtful, Hillary. You should give him a chance. You guys could be a real good team if you worked together. I just have this feeling about it." I scowled at her like she was nuts.

"No-no way," I replied.

"Alright. I'm not going to force you," she continued. "If you do change your mind, and I hope you do, you'll have to tell me the reason. Otherwise, that means you're not ready."

"Don't get your hopes up. I ain't changing my mind," I said.

"It's your loss, and his, too," she commented, sort of in an off-handed way. My arms stayed folded across my chest and I stared at the wall. I wasn't workin' with Jackson. Period.

And it made me mad that Mrs. Lorrey thought we should be a team. What a stupid idea.

Chapter Eight

The Rambler

"Okay, class," said Mrs. Price, "we're going to get into our pairings and start working on our science project."

It was after lunch, and I hadn't paid no attention to Jackson all day. I was still mad at him. But I did watch him from a distance and decided he likes to be alone. He don't really try to hang around no one. Of course, he don't know no one that good, so maybe that's why.

I went over to his desk. "Alright, so what are we workin' on?" I asked. I forgot, but remembered that it began with P.

"Pottos. They begin with P," he said. "And guess what? Their sub-family is Perodicticinae and their genus is Perodicticus, which both begin with P. That will help our grade on the pottos."

"Great," I said with a half smile. What was I supposed to say? I didn't have no clue what he was talking about, but it sounded good. I thought about telling him that Mrs. Price may not actually like P better than any other letter but I didn't get around to it.

"I looked up some information on the Internet last night. That's how I know about the genus and subfamily. I was on our computer for twenty-seven minutes," he said before I could tell him about my P joke.

"Good," I said.

"That means you have to do twenty-seven minutes of work, be-cause Mrs. Price said you have to do fair share time," Jackson noted.

"So are you timing me?" I asked. I didn't have to put up with that.

"Well, we have to keep track of our work time so you can do fair share. That's what Mrs. Price said," he answered. I couldn't believe it.

"Well, I spent twenty-eight minutes trying to draw the potto. It came out okay, but I want to try to make it better," I said. Now that was a lie, a bold-faced lie. I didn't even know what pottos looked like.

"Oh, well, then I need to do my fair share," he said very matter-of-factly. "You did more than me." He opened up a notebook, which had both our names written in it and wrote twenty-eight minutes by my name and twenty-seven by his. I shook my head.

"Now, class," Mrs. Price said, "I've made arrangements for us to visit the library. There are several computers in there, so you can take turns. And, of course, there are a lot of encyclopedias and other reference books."

"Mrs. Price, I really don't feel good," said Pamela. "Can I go to the nurse?"

"No," said Mrs. Price. My ears perked up. "You and Jenny will work nicely, and I mean *very* nicely, together in the library." She looked right at Pamela the whole time she talked. Her voice was stern. I wondered if she knew Pamela was calling Jenny "Healthy" behind her back.

Interesting, I thought.

Everyone gathered their things and got in line, but for some reason Jackson had to be last. He wouldn't let no one get behind him. Then when we got to the library, he sat at a table and didn't do nothin' 'cause he wanted to use the computer first but it was already taken. Seems to me that if you're gonna be last in line, you won't get your first pick. Jackson don't think about these kinds of things, I guess.

"You don't need to use the computer here, if you got one at home," I said to him.

"I don't have one at home. I have three. One for my mom and dad, one for me, and one for my sister."

"So why do you need to use the one in the library?" I asked. He scrunched his eyebrows and frowned.

"Because," he said. Now there's a good reason. Not!

"Do you have a computer at home?" he asked.

"Why?" I shot back. I wasn't ready to tell him that I didn't have one. I don't want no one at school to know the things I don't have. I'd be the laughing stock. I faked everything I had. Video games, cable TV, a DVD player – you name it – people thought I had it. I don't want no one makin' fun of me just 'cause we're poor and don't got nothin'.

"Why?" he mimicked me exactly, even in how his voice went up. I didn't have no idea how his brain worked, 'cause then he asked, "Why do you have a computer at home?" He crinkled his forehead and had the most serious look. I was confused. We wasn't communicating, that's for sure. But at least I didn't have to lie.

"Because," I said, smiling. It was the same answer he gave to me a minute ago. Didn't make no sense, but that didn't seem to matter. And it wasn't a lie.

"I'm goin' over to get an encyclopedia," I said.

"I'm waiting to use the computer," Jackson answered.

"You'll be waiting a while." I got up, walked over to the encyclopedias, selected the P volume, and brought it back to the table. "You know," I said, "I'm racking up minutes on your little fair share time sheet. You're gonna have a lot to make up."

"I'm waiting to use the computer for my fair share," he answered. I turned the pages of the book to "potto" and studied the picture.

"Look. Ain't he the cutest thing you ever seen?" I said, shoving the book to Jackson. He was a really cute little animal with big, brown eyes. I was gonna like drawing him.

"I thought you drew him last night for twenty-eight minutes. So that meant you saw him last night," he said.

"Yeah, I did," I lied. "I was just pointing out how cute he was."

"Oh, well. Look," he said. Then he counted the lines in the article and announced, "There are twelve lines. If each line has eight words, that's ninety-six words. On the computer last night, I found three articles, and I bet if I did the word count, it would be way more than ninety-six. I don't like encyclopedias as much as I like computers."

"Well, I like this picture," I said.

"They have better ones on the computer, and they have more than one. I didn't count them, but I can, and there are a lot."

"I don't care. I like this one," I insisted. I wasn't gonna be pushed around. Then Jackson proceeded to tell me all this information he learned about the potto. There was NO stopping him. He rambled on and on. I was tired of hearing about their diet and their habitat, but no matter what I did, Jackson just continued talking non-stop. He musta spent way more than twenty-seven minutes studyin' pottos, as much as he knew. Finally, I did what I had to do. I grabbed him on the arm and told him to stop. Just like I expected, he jumped. Now was my chance to find out about what I really wanted to know.

"Jackson," I said, and then snapped my fingers in front of his face to make sure I had his attention. "Where do you live?" I couldn't believe he actually lived in the same apartments as me. I wanted to know if he was poor, too.

"I live in the Westwater Apartment complex on North Mason Drive," he said.

"Why don't you live in a house?" I asked. That's what someone asked me when I first moved here.

"I don't live in a house, but I will," he answered in his strange way.

"Yeah, I will too some day," I said, sort of wishfully.

"Well, I won't live in a house Sunday, but I will in three months and sixteen days." That was a goofy answer. I didn't really get it. Then he smiled and asked, "Do you want to hear about my house?" Honestly, I was a little curious, but thought he might start rambling on again, so I said no.

"Well, it's three thousand two hundred square feet and sits on a lot that's one point eight nine acres. That's only eleven one hundredths of an acre short of two acres, which is what the size of our lot in ..."

"Jackson," I whispered real loud, "STOP."

"Okay, but it is not built yet so we have to stay in apartments. My apartment is the biggest one they have. But it is only two thousand square feet. My room is fourteen feet by fourteen feet, which is ..."

"Jackson!" This time I just lightly touched his arm. "I ain't tryin' to be mean, but you talk too much," I said. He pulled his arm away, crinkled his forehead and sort of frowned.

"We need to get on the computer," he commented. I slipped a

piece of paper from my notebook and started drawing the potto from the encyclopedia.

So he lived in the apartments 'cause he was waitin' for a big, beautiful house to be built. In other words, he ain't poor. Not like me.

I ignored him for the rest of library time. He kept griping about getting on the computer. It got on my nerves. I decided for sure I wasn't doing no research. Computer King Jackson could do it. He already knew everything anyways.

Chapter Nine

The Bus Seat

Wednesday was finally over. Me and Jenny was sitting together in the third seat back on the bus. I was by the window, and she was by the aisle. It was a good place to see everyone come in.

The bus driver, Mr. Bill, sat in his seat and greeted everyone with a big

"How ya' doing?" and "Move on back and find yourself a seat," or something like that. Most all kids like Mr. Bill. He's a friendly man and real nice.

Me and Jenny ignored him for a while. We had stuff to talk about.

"I hate working with Pamela," she said. "Do you know how many times a day she calls me Healthy and then says oops and apologizes?"

"Tell the teacher," I said. Jenny shook her head. She was right. It wouldn't do no good. Even if the teacher believed her, Pamela would get her in the end. She was good at being mean, and sneaky, too.

"Jackson's the one that started it," I said, thinking about what he done when he "complimented" Jenny.

"Well, at least he apologized," Jenny said.

"Not really," I disagreed. "He wouldn't have said sorry if his mom didn't make him."

"But I still think he meant it," she insisted.

"Whatever. He shouldn't have said nothin' in the first place. We both know that." That was my final word on the subject. We was silent for a little, until Jenny saw him.

"Look," she said, pointing at the front of the bus.

"Hello, son, you must be the new kid," said Mr. Bill. "Just move on back and find yourself a seat. There's plenty of kids on this bus who'd like to meet you."

"Yes, this is my first day on the bus," Jackson said. And then he just stood there and looked at the front passenger seat.

"Go on, son, move on back," Mr. Bill repeated.

"I'm supposed to sit there," said Jackson, pointing at the seat right behind the driver.

"Now, son, we don't have assigned seats here, and it looks like that one is already taken." Mr. Bill was trying to be nice.

"I have an assigned seat right there," said Jackson. He just stood and stared at the seat.

"Go on," Mr. Bill said gently, "move on back."

"I can sit there and we'll have three in the seat," suggested Jackson. He smiled, like it was a good idea and would solve the problem. Then he added, "It's a good plan, because sometimes bus seats hold three kids."

"Your instructions are to move to the back of the bus," said Mr. Bill. He was more firm this time but still nice. Jackson stepped closer to the seat.

"We can have three kids in this seat. Do you want me to show you?" Jackson asked, like Mr. Bill had just agreed with his plan. Mr. Bill leaned back, put his arm between Jackson and the seat, and spoke.

"Young man, you haven't told me yet. What is your name?"

"Jackson Evan Thomas. My initials are J-E-T, and they spell jet."

"Well, Jackson, I want you to understand that you have to move back. Once a seat is taken, you can't have it. Those are the rules on this bus." He looked at Jackson, and Jackson looked at the seat.

"Well, I thought the rules said you could have three in a seat. Those were the rules on my old bus," Jackson explained.

"Jackson, listen carefully. You're starting to skate on thin ice. You really are, and you need to find a new seat now."

"No, I'm not," Jackson answered, very matter-of-factly.

"You are, and you will have to get off this bus if you don't move to a new seat." Jackson stood there. There was a long pause, and then he said the funniest thing, even though it wasn't no time to be joking.

"Is that an idiom? Because the temperature has to be below thirty-two degrees for there to be ice. It was forty-five degrees this morning and the weatherman predicted that it would get up to fifty-eight degrees by this afternoon. It's impossible for there to be ice, and I don't have on skates. It doesn't make sense, so is that an idiom?" Mr. Bill looked at him like he was nuts or something.

"Geez," he said under his breath. "Nobody said a word about him. Wonder what his problem is."

"Oh," Jackson said, like Mr. Bill actually wanted an answer, "I know my problem. I'm supposed to sit in the front seat behind the driver, but you won't let me. I can sit there, if you let three be in the seat, and then there won't be a problem. Okay?"

Mr. Bill stared at him. Finally, he spoke.

"I don't think you get it. Let me be clear. You will not be sitting in this seat today." He turned and touched the front seat. "You will be sitting in a seat back there." He pointed to the empty seats in back of the bus. "Now, you have three to get going, or you will not ride this bus today."

Jackson stood there; his fists slowly moved up to his chest. He started twisting them back and forth right under his chin. Then he unleashed his fingers from his fists and started rubbing them together. He stared at them.

"One," said Mr. Bill after Jackson didn't move.

"My mom said this bus would be the same as my old bus, except the bus number would be different. She said I'm supposed to ride the bus today. She's not going to pick me up today," Jackson muttered.

"Two," said Mr. Bill.

"I have to sit in the front seat. Then it will be the same as my old bus. I like the front seat. This bus is supposed to be the same as my old bus except for the number," he continued.

"Three," said Mr. Bill.

"I have to ride the bus. My mom is not picking me up," Jackson insisted. He tried to sit in the front seat, but that's when Mr. Bill stood up, right between Jackson and the seat. Jackson was blocked. Mr. Bill looked out among the rest of us and chose Jenny.

"Jenny, would you please run inside the school and tell someone I need help out here." She nodded her head, stood up, and headed off the bus.

"Jackson, you can still stay on the bus if you go to the back. You simply cannot sit in a seat that has already been taken," repeated Mr. Bill. I think he was trying to give him a chance.

But Jackson wasn't listening. He looked like he was having an attack or something. His knees was like little springs, going up and down real fast. It was like he was standing and rocking at the same time. His fingers was squiggling back and forth in front of his chest, and he was looking straight down at them. Mr. Bill put his hand on Jackson's back, but he jerked away.

"Son," Mr. Bill said. He was trying to be nice. "I really want you to ride the bus, but you must understand there are rules."

"I don't like the rules." I think that's what Jackson muttered. But he was very quiet, and he couldn't get out of that weird rocking position he was in. His face was getting red. And then I saw big tears drip onto his fingers. I looked away 'cause I didn't like that.

Jenny finally got back to the bus. She edged herself around Jackson and sat down. We watched Jackson and Mr. Bill, and so did everyone else.

The principal and Mrs. Price and Mrs. Lorrey got there right after Jenny. They was able to get Jackson to walk out of the bus. But it was hard. Mrs. Lorrey had a file card with "bus" written on it. She crossed it out with a marker and said it was coming off today's schedule. That was kind of odd. "Whatever," I thought. In my opinion, it was ridiculous how upset Jackson got. All for a dumb seat.

"What do you think is wrong with him?" asked Jenny.

"I don't know," I said.

"Maybe that's where he sat in his other school. He probably just can't change," she guessed.

"That ain't a choice," I answered. "You just gotta change with the school. That's just the way it is. It's easy. I've done it a million times."

"It might be easy for you, but not for Jackson. I feel sorry for him," she said.

"Why?" I shot back. "He's just stubborn. That's all."

"Maybe, but still, I'd hate to be that way," she commented, sort of to herself more than to me.

When the bus pulled away, Jackson was standing on the sidewalk with Mrs. Lorrey on one side and Mrs. Price on the other. I hoped he didn't find out what I was doing for our science report – nothin' but a picture. I'd hate for him to have another fit like he did on the bus. It really bothered me, seeing that fit. And it made me think of something I'd never thought about before.

What did people think about me when I had temper tantrums? I hoped I didn't look like him. That would be embarrassing.

Chapter Ten

Promises, Promises

I t was ten o'clock. I laid my head on the pillow and listened to the silence of our dark apartment. I hated it. I wished Grandma could be here again. At least that was somebody. Slowly my mind drifted off, but I didn't sleep.

I was thinking about Jackson. Even though he was odd, he was sort of interesting. When my mom called earlier, he's all I talked about. I even told her that he lived in our apartments, but not how I spied on him and his family. She wouldn't have liked that.

"Well," she said, "that's nice that you're working on the same project and live in the same apartments. Would you like to invite him over this weekend?"

"No, not really," I answered. She didn't know that everyone thought I had lots of things, like computers and stuff. If Jackson found out what I don't have and told on me, my whole class would find out I was poor. That was a secret I didn't want no one to know.

We talked a while more. Then I hung up and headed out to the swings. I was pumping myself really high into the air when I heard a slamming sound in the distance and a loud, angry voice. I looked and seen Jackson's sister headed my way. Her arms was folded across her chest, and she looked just plain mad. When she got over to the playground, she went to the farthest swing away from me and sat there, not moving. I was glad I decided to talk to her, 'cause I found out some real interesting stuff.

"Hey, you new to this place?" I called to her across the swings.

"Yeah," she answered. I dragged my feet on the ground and slowed up on the swing.

"What's your name?" I asked.

"I'm Elizabeth. But mostly people call me Liz."

"Nice to meet you."

"Thanks." Then silence.

"Which apartment do you live in?" I asked.

"Over there," she pointed, "Apartment Building A. We're staying there till our house gets built."

"You're lucky. Those are the nice ones," I said. "They have three or four bedrooms, don't they?"

"Yep." Silence again. I stopped swinging completely, moved over to the swing beside her, and sat down. Then I tried to find out more stuff.

"You got any brothers or sisters?"

"I got a whacky brother who we all cater to." She wasn't smilin' or jokin', as far as I could tell.

"Really?" I said. I wanted to hear more.

"Oh yeah," she answered, and then she started to open up. "If I could tell you the stuff my mom does for him, you wouldn't believe it. She caters to his every need from computers to weather to eating. She even counts out snacks in sets of five. How nutty is that?"

"Pretty nutty," I agreed.

"She makes out a schedule for him every day 'cause he can't just go with the flow. He gets crazy if things aren't just the way he expects them to be."

"My mom never makes out schedules for me," I said.

"That's 'cause you're normal," she said. I took it as a compliment. Then she continued, "Guess what happened today."

"What?"

"Well, he couldn't ride the bus 'cause of some kind of trouble he caused, and then my mom calls the school to say it's not his fault." She let out a sigh. "Nothing's ever his fault. It's ridiculous!"

"So that's what you're mad about?" I asked. She seemed real mad.

"Well, normally I wouldn't care, but today was different."

"Why?" I asked.

"Because I got in trouble for pointing out that nothing's his fault. My mom lets him get away with everything." Then Liz tells me they just moved from Illinois and how hard it has been on Jackson, according to her mom.

"But what about me?" she says.

She went on to tell me that she's in the middle of eleventh grade and had left all these friends back at her other school. Her mom just frets about Jackson all the time. I guess Jackson is a little like his dad, so his dad don't worry about him. I think his dad is a computer whiz or something, according to what I could figure out.

Anyways, I sort of liked Liz. Her and her mom got in a big fight, and she told her mom off. So her mom told her to go to her room, and that's when she stormed out the front door and came over to the playground. Sounds like something I'd do.

"So why's your mom so worried about your brother all the time?" I asked.

"Haven't you been listening?" She seemed a little mad. "He's weird! He can't help it. And my mom just can't let it go. She's always on the Internet or reading books to find out some new way to help him."

"Oh," I said. This time I was silent.

"There's a reason he's weird," Liz added after a minute.

"What's that?" I asked.

"Not allowed to tell. I promised, and one thing I don't do is break my promises."

"Oh," I said again and then added, "He don't have a disease or nothing, does he?" I didn't want to be catchin' nothin' from him.

"Of course not, and I already told you I'm not allowed to tell. So don't ask."

"Sorry," I said and started swinging a little.

"What are you, third grade? Something like that?" she asked me after a short while. People always think I'm young 'cause I'm so little. Plus my hair is frizzy. Plus my clothes ain't that great. I get used stuff mostly, but sometimes I'll get something brand new.

"I'm actually older than that, but I ain't tellin'." I didn't want her to know I knew Jackson. Then I copied what she said earlier, exactly, word for word, "Not allowed to tell. I promised, and one thing I don't do is break my promises." Liz started laughing, and then I did, too.

"You're bad!" she said. "If you were talking to my brother, he'd be totally confused."

"Really? He don't get jokes?"

"Nope. And he sure doesn't tell them. At least none that are any good." She shook her head back and forth. She was quite serious.

I wondered what that meant. Was all those great jokes I thought he was telling actually not jokes? I'd have to go back and rethink everything that happened over the last couple of days.

"How about you? You got any brothers or sisters," Liz asked.

"Nope. It's just me."

"You're lucky," she said.

"I don't think so," I replied. "Sometimes I think it would be nice to have someone to play with."

"Well, I can guarantee it's not that great. Sometimes I hate having a brother. He's practically all my mom thinks about, and it's just not fair." I didn't say nothin'.

"And that's what I'm gonna tell her that when I go back in," she added. I wondered what her mom would do. I wondered why her mom always thought about Jackson. I wondered about them for a long time.

○ ○ ○

And then – just like that – I snapped out of my thoughts. I could hear Mom unlocking the door to our apartment, opening it, shutting it, and then locking it up again.

"I'm home!" she called. It was time for me to start the routine I had grown to love so much.

I rolled over on my side toward the window, pulled the covers over my head, and pretended to be asleep. Mom cracked open the door and said, "Hey Silly-Hilly, you awake?" I didn't move. So she came over, pulled the covers back off my face, and kissed me on the cheek.

"I love you so much, Hill, and I'm gonna make things better for us. I promise." Then she pulled the covers up over my shoulders again and rubbed my back for a few minutes. She hummed my favorite lullaby from when I was a little kid.

I smiled, 'cause this time I really, really believed her. She ain't had a drink ever since we moved to Grandma's. And she didn't have no new boyfriends that I hated. And she didn't get fired from her job. And she didn't quit.

That's 'cause she loved me. And she was working real hard to make our life better.

Chapter Eleven

On Base

"Go Hillary, go!" I could hear Jenny and some other kids cheerin' for me.

We was at recess havin' races, and I was runnin' my heart out 'cause I wanted to beat Pamela, who was pretty fast, too. She was real fast. She was beatin' me, but I was ready to pass her when we reached the finish. But it was too late, and she won.

I was so MAD!

I shooed off Jenny and a few others who tried to tell me what a good race it was. I ain't lost a race that I wanted to win in a long time, and I sure shouldn't have lost this one. There wasn't nothin' good about it.

I wandered off to the big tree by the old monkey bars we didn't use no more and sat down against it. That's when I noticed Jackson. He was walkin' along the edge of the playground all by hisself lookin' at the ground. Every once in a while, he'd stop, look at some kids, and just watch them. Then he'd look at the ground again and start walkin'. How the heck did he think he was gonna make friends doin' that? Maybe he didn't care.

"Hey, Hillary!" I turned. It was Paul. Perfect Paul. He actually is perfect for real 'cause he don't get on my nerves and he gets straight A's, but he don't act like he's better than everybody else.

"Yeah," I answered. If he told me what a great race I ran, I'd run him off, too, like I did everybody else. I turned back to Jackson and watched him. Now he was lookin' up at the sky.

"We're gettin' a game of kickball going. You wanna play?" Paul asked.

"Nope."

"Come on. We need some more people," Paul begged.

"Look out there," I said, pointing at Jackson. "He ain't doin' nothin' but lookin' at the sky. Why don't you ask him?" So that's what he did.

"Jackson!" Paul yelled, as he jogged toward him. Jackson looked at Paul, and then started doin' somethin' really weird. He lifted his hands up in front of his chest and started squiggling his fingers real fast. I ain't ever seen anything so strange in my life. He just kept doin' that until Paul finally reached him.

I kept watchin' Jackson's hands while the two of them talked. He squiggled his fingers a little longer, then stopped when he started following Paul over to the kickball field, which is actually a baseball field. They was passing me up, and Paul wasn't sayin' nothin'. But Jackson was just a yammerin' away about the clouds. That musta been what he was lookin' at when he was watchin' the sky.

"See, the cirrostratus clouds are formed from the cirrus clouds that gather together," he explained. Paul looked like he was trying to flag someone down at the kickball field, but that didn't bother Jackson in the least. He just kept on going, "There were a lot of cirrus clouds about forty-three minutes ago. I saw them from the window during spelling. Now they're forming into the cirrostratus clouds. Possibly, a layer of altostratus clouds will hide them later on. How this happens is ..." And on and on he went, or so it seemed, but I couldn't hear. They kept walkin' toward the ball field, which was a ways off.

I don't know why, but I wanted to see them, so I climbed up onto the old monkey bars to watch. We wasn't allowed to be on those monkey bars because they wasn't safe, or at least that's what the teachers told us. But I didn't care.

When it was Jackson's turn to kick, he stood beside the plate with his hands pretending he was holding a bat. There was a bunch of yelling, and then someone showed him how to stand behind the plate to get ready to kick the ball. The pitcher rolled the kickball across the ground pretty hard, and Jackson totally missed. He swung his leg too late and too slow, lost his balance, and fell on his butt. From where I was, it looked kind of funny, and there was lots of laughin'. Paul went over, gave Jackson his hand, and pulled him up. Looked like he even gave him a thumbs-up. That was dumb. A thumbs-up for fallin' on your butt don't make no sense to me.

Then came the second toss. Jackson was back to squiggling his fingers, but they were at his sides this time, and they stopped as soon as he kicked. The squiggling might have helped a little, because at least this time the ball touched his foot. It went foul, but I don't think he knew about fouls, 'cause he ran to first base and just stood there. Everyone was yelling at him to go back to home plate. Finally, someone went up to him and pointed to where he should go. Jackson started to walk back. He frowned and shook his head back and forth and walked real slow.

"Hillary, you know better than that," came the voice of Mrs. Eastland. "Get down right now." She was the playground supervisor.

"Sorry, I forgot," I fibbed. I jumped off the forbidden monkey bars and headed towards the game.

Jackson had just gotten back to home plate when I plopped myself down on the ground several yards from the sidelines and not near no one. The ball was rolling toward Jackson, and he just stood there in its way. It bounced off the bottom of his legs and headed out toward the infield. I don't know why, but that's when he kicked at it. Of course, he missed by a mile. Still, it was a fair play because the ball got into the field. It was also an easy out.

But Jackson ran to first base and stood there again. Everyone was telling him he was out and to get off the field, so he finally did. He was passin' me up, headed somewhere, when I decided to talk to him.

"Hey, Jackson," I called. He kept on walking.

"Jackson!" I yelled louder. He still kept on walking.

"JACKSON!" I hollered, loud enough for the world to hear. He finally stopped, kind of jerked his head, and looked around a little. But not at me.

"Over here," I called. Finally, he saw me.

"Where you goin'?" I asked.

"Out there." He pointed to the edge of the playground in the direction he had been walking.

"Ain't you gonna finish the game?" I asked.

"I'm out."

"But you're not out of the game. You're just out at bat," I explained. Maybe they didn't play kickball where he came from.

"I didn't bat," he said.

"You know what I mean," I answered.

He shook his head. "I don't want to play. Everybody yells at me, and I don't like it."

"Yeah, yeah, yeah, that's how these snotty kids are at this rich school," I replied. He didn't hear me, I guess, 'cause he changed the subject.

"Did you see me get on base. I got on base two times." His finger was pointing up and he was smiling. "I never got on base before."

"But you didn't get on base," I answered. "You got out."

"I was on the base. I was on two times."

"It don't count as being on base if you get out," I tried to explain. He thought for a few seconds.

"But I only got out one time. So that must mean I got on base one time," he reasoned, if that's what you want to call it. It was actually more like the opposite of reasoning to me.

"Don't they play kickball where you come from?" I asked. I ain't ever felt so frustrated tryin' to explain a simple thing to somebody.

"I don't know if they play it at Westwater Apartments. I never did," he said. Geez, he was a real piece of work.

"Noooooooooooo," I said stretching it out as long as I could. "I mean in Illinois. Ain't that where you came from?"

"Oh," he said. "Yeah, we played it. But I didn't. I didn't like the ball coming at me. I still don't, but I have to try to join in when people invite me. That's the rule."

"What rule?" I asked.

"It's the rule about how to make friends when you move to a new place. I learned rules for how to make friends, and sometimes I forget to use them, but not this time," he said. "Also, I shouldn't talk too much about weather or monkeys, but I forget that rule sometimes. But if I talk too much about that stuff and say more than three things without letting someone else talk, then ..."

The whistle blew, thank heavens. I stood up and ran to the blacktop.

I wonder if Jackson knew about my rules: I wouldn't do no work on the potto report, except the picture. And I wouldn't be in no group with him when I went to see Mrs. Lorrey.

Maybe I'd be nice to him. At least I'd try. But only if he didn't hurt Jenny no more, like he did the first day.

Chapter 12

Off, A Little

"I worked thirty-one minutes last night on my pottos report," Jackson announced. "How long did you work?" He had his little notebook out so he could write down our times.

"Thirty-three minutes," I fibbed.

"Okay, so that means you worked one minute longer than me Wednesday, six minutes longer than me Thursday, and two minutes longer today, so you're up to nine minutes more than me." I nodded, but wanted to roll my eyes. I kept remembering what his sister said: He don't get jokes. I was startin' to believe it.

Clap-clap, pause, clap-clap-clap. Mrs. Price used her little first-grade method to get our attention. We all got quiet and dutifully clapped the same way, like a bunch of little robots. Except Jackson. That was kind of cool. He sat there and didn't do it. I was giving him a thumbs-up in my mind until he totally messed up.

Clap-clap, pause, clap-clap-clap. He clapped kind of loud, and it was way after everyone else.

Silence. Dead silence

And then we all started laughing. Jackson looked around and finally joined in. Through the noise, I could hear Mrs. Price counting backwards from ten. That was bad. If she got down to zero, we would lose recess. Quickly, the class got quiet – except for Jackson. He didn't stop until someone poked him and told him what to do.

"Class, we'll be working in the library on our science reports today. The computers are down, so you'll only have the books and reference materials to work with, along with your own research. Now, everyone, line up with your partners."

We gathered our stuff, and just like every other time we lined up, Jackson wanted to be last.

"Why do you always want to be last?" I asked on the way down to the library. He didn't say nothin', so I tried again.

"Well," he replied after long wait. "I don't like it when people bump me and step on my shoes."

"Oh," I said. It made total sense to me, 'cause one thing's for sure, he don't like being touched.

When we got to the library, the tables was all set up with six chairs at each one. Me and Jackson sat with Jenny and Pamela and Evy and Claudia. That's 'cause Jenny saved a seat for me, and Evy and Claudia was real good friends with Pamela. Jenny and me called them the mean girls.

"Lucky us, huh?" I said to Jenny, then rolled my eyes.

"Yeah," she whispered back. "But that's okay. We've got a lot of work to do."

"Not me," I declared quietly, "I just got to draw a picture of ..."

"Excuse me, please. I'm your partner. I think the teacher said you're supposed to talk your partner. That's me," Jackson interrupted. I just pretended like I didn't hear him.

"I just gotta draw a picture of a potto," I continued, making sure to face Jenny. "They are so cute. Have you ever seen one?"

"Nah, but that reminds me, could you draw a picture of a koala for my project?"

"Okay, but I need something so I can ..." Interrupted again, only louder this time.

"Excuse me, please. I think you're supposed to be talking to me. That's what the teacher said. I'm your science partner, and we're supposed to talk about our potto report," Jackson blurted.

Evy, Claudia, and Pamela started giggling. I couldn't even have a simple conversation with Jenny without him interrupting and that burned me. If a glare could kill, Jackson would have died right on the spot. Everyone knows my mad look. Everyone. I turned and gave him the most hateful eyes I could, turned my back on him, and started talking to Jenny again.

"I need a picture or something to be able to draw it right."

"Okay," she answered, "but let's talk about it later. We need ..." This time it was Pamela who interrupted.

"Excuse me, please. You're supposed to be talking to me. I'm your science partner. We're supposed to talk about our koala report." She mimicked Jackson's voice exactly. That got Evy and Claudia laughing again, but I wasn't laughing at no joke Pamela made.

I stood up and slammed my chair to the table loud enough for everyone to know I was mad, but soft enough so I wouldn't get in trouble. Then I headed over to the reference books. I turned around and saw idiot Jackson followin' me. He ain't got a clue when it comes to taking a hint.

"LEAVE ME ALONE!" I yelled in my loudest whisper. He squinted his eyes, scrunched up his forehead, started squiggling his fingers, and after a long moment, turned around and went back to the table.

I let out a long sigh of relief, rested my elbows on the bookshelf, and watched my table. They was happy without me. Everyone talking, then laughing, then talking, then laughing. But Jackson was a little off rhythm, like he didn't know when to laugh. He would start laughin' after everyone else and keep on laughin' after everyone had stopped. Kind of like what happened with the clapping in class earlier.

It all came to an end when Mrs. Price headed toward them. Like magic, everyone got to work except Jackson. He got two pencils and started flicking them back and forth. He was hypnotizing himself, I think, 'cause he just kept staring at those flicking pencils.

Meanwhile, I got busy, too. I found the "P" encyclopedia and flipped through it to find a picture of a potto. I wanted the librarian to copy it for me on the copy machine. She did, but since she was busy, it took a few minutes. By the time I got back to my seat, I had calmed down.

"Hey, Jackson," I whispered, "sorry about earlier. I was just mad." I could hear Evy and Claudia giggling, but ignored them.

"Look," I said, "I got a picture of a potto." He looked, but didn't say nothing.

"I'm going to take it home and draw it tonight." His face crinkled up and he looked confused.

"It's gonna be real good," I promised. It would be, 'cause I thought pottos was real cute so I wanted to do a good drawing. Finally, he said what was on his mind.

"I thought you already drew the potto. You told me you did."

He was right, according to the little fib I told him earlier. That's the problem with telling lies. You gotta remember 'em all to keep track.

"Yeah, but did I tell you my dog ate the picture?" I said. Another dumb lie. I wished I could take that one back, 'cause then we got into this big, long talk about dogs. Actually, it was him talkin' and me hardly sayin' nothing. What kinda dog did I have? He had such and such a kind and blah, blah, blah. Finally, after many nice tries and hints, I just told him straight up what the situation was.

"We can't talk about dogs no more. We gotta do our potto report."

And he listened. Right away, he started talking about the potto spine.

That's when I it dawned on me – Jackson's just a little off when it comes to taking hints. He didn't get my mad-face look earlier and he didn't get my nice tries to change the subject just now. It's better to tell him just like it is. Then he gets it.

As strange as it may seem, I was very interested in the potto spine. It can be dangerous. Me and Jackson was actually having a real conversation about it when we both jumped about a mile.

"So how's it going?" Mrs. Price asked, gently touching our backs. I never saw her coming, and I don't think Jackson did either.

"I'm sorry, I didn't mean to startle you," she said.

"That's okay," I replied. "We're doing fine."

"Are you both working hard?" she asked.

"Yes, m'am," I said in my most dutiful voice.

"Actually, Hillary has spent nine more minutes than me on the potto report. Each day, we tabulate our time. I need to put in extra time this weekend, so I can do my fair share."

"Wow! That's impressive, Hillary. I'm really proud of you. Wait until Mrs. Lorry hears," beamed Mrs. Price.

I gave her a lame smile and wondered about Jackson. He actually thought I was a good science partner? I couldn't believe it. And he even gave me a compliment to the teacher. There ain't nobody that's ever done that before.

Maybe he don't know about me 'cause he's off a little. But that's okay. In fact, I think I like that about him.

He don't try to figure me out all the time. And he don't judge me. That's hard to do, 'cause no matter how much I want to be, I know I ain't that good. But Jackson, I think he likes me how I am, or at least how he thinks I am. That's cool.

If only I could really be that way.

Chapter Thirteen

Too Many Lies

It was good news! Mom was getting off early. She said we was goin' out to dinner, too. What a great start to a weekend.

I swang high into the sky thinkin' about where I wanted to eat. Chinese or pizza or burgers. It was my choice and

I hadn't ate out in a long time so anything would be good. That's when I saw Elizabeth coming over. She waved at me from a distance and kind of jogged over.

"Hi," she said.

"How ya' doing?" I yelled from the peak of my swing. I was as far forward and high up as I was going to get.

"Fine. You know what I forgot to ask you the other day," she called out, "your name. I forgot to ask your name."

"Hillary," I answered. This time my swing had me as far back as I was going to get.

"Hillary?" she said in a great big, stunned voice. I could hear a question in how she said it.

"Yeah, Hillary."

"Are you in fifth grade?" she asked in that same voice. She was gonna figure out that I knew Jackson. I could tell.

"Yep. Mrs. Price is my teacher." I just laid it right out there. My feet dragged the ground to slow my swinging. She sat down on the swing next to me and moved around in circles with her feet on the ground, but didn't say nothin'. Finally, she spoke.

"So you know my brother Jackson." It was a statement, not a question. Not at all.

"Yep."

"And you knew who he was the other day when I was complaining about him." A statement again.

"Yep." I wasn't gonna apologize.

"Why didn't you tell me?"

"You didn't ask." I hoped I was right. I couldn't remember exactly word for word everything we was talkin' about.

"Well, it just wasn't nice of you. You should have said something," she said.

"Why? Why does it matter?" I asked.

"It just wasn't honest," she shot back. I thought about it. It wasn't no lie. I never said I didn't know Jackson. So it was no big deal. That's what I told her.

"If you don't understand, well, never mind," she shot back angrily, and then she stood up to leave.

"Wait!" I called when I saw her turn and start walking away. I don't know why, but I wanted her to understand.

"The reason I didn't say nothing is 'cause ... well, like you said, he ain't just right, and I wanted to know about him." She turned around and looked at me with her eyebrows scrunched together like Jackson does. Her mouth was all pulled over to one side.

"I thought you wouldn't tell me nothin' important if I told you I knew him." She kept lookin' at me with that same look.

"It helped what you told me about him," I offered. Still quiet.

"I had a better day with him today. You know what I like about him? He don't judge people. He just believes 'em." I was tryin' real hard to be nice. Finally, she spoke.

"Were you following us down the sidewalk the other day?" I could feel butterflies in my stomach. Did she KNOW that was me, or did she just THINK it was?

"When?" I asked. It was a stalling tactic.

"That would be Tuesday," she answered, almost with a snotty sound. "Some kid was following us. Could have been a girl or a boy. Had on a Seattle Seahawks ball cap." Phew! Good. I could tell she didn't know it was me.

"Sorry, I don't have no Seattle ball cap, and I go to my dad's on Tuesday." That was a good excuse, even though I got no idea who my dad is and prob'ly ain't ever gonna meet him.

"Well, someone was following us. I was just thinking it was you."

I shook my head no, and she sat down on the swing again.

"Anyways," she continued, "the real reason I came over was to straighten out what I said about my brother the other day. I wasn't really fair to him."

"Oh?" I asked, wondering what she meant.

"I was just mad," she continued.

"Well, you was right about one thing," I commented.

"What's that?" she asked.

"I ain't tryin' to be mean," I said to soften what I was going to say, "but he seems like he's spoiled, 'cause he gets to sit on the same bus seat that he had the big hissy fit about on Wednesday."

"He's not really spoiled. I just didn't explain him very well," she responded. I didn't say nothin' but I didn't really believe her either.

"He'll be in a different bus seat soon. He's working on it. You'll see," she said, like she knew what I was thinking.

"He's workin' on it? What's that s'posed to mean? I would've been kicked off the bus for a week if I done what he done."

"That's 'cause you're norm ... I mean, not like he is. You're a different person than him," she said. That comment just hit me as so funny.

"Well duh!" I giggled. "Jackson and I ain't the same person. You must be Einstein." Liz started laughing, too.

"Yeah. I'm known for being a genius. Especially, for knowing that different people aren't the same." We laughed a little longer and then she started again.

"You know, and this is not a joke, Jackson really is like Einstein in some ways." I looked at Liz like she was nuts.

"Yeah, I'm sure," I said, shaking my head.

"No, really," she continued. "You should see how much he knows about some things. It's unbelievable." She sorta had my attention. I already could tell he was way, way smart on pottos and tornadoes.

"Sometimes he reads encyclopedias," she continued. "But mostly he reads technical magazines and stuff on the Internet, things like that." She stopped for a moment, but then added, "He's really, really smart. I'm not kiddin'. Like Einstein."

"That's sorta interesting," I said and I meant it.

"I even got him to do most of my report for me last year on tornadoes. I got an A on it." She smiled when she spoke. "Yeah, he's kind of good to have for a brother sometimes. Nobody I know could claim their little brother did a report for them. And got them an A."

"That's true." I said. Then I added, "I'm doing a report with him now on the potto."

"Yeah, I know. I don't even know why you're doing all that work on it. He knows so much about pottos, it's ridiculous. He's all into monkeys and primates and stuff like that."

"I ain't done that much," I blurted out and then wanted to take it back. Sometimes I have such a big mouth.

"That's not what he says. He's got you timed down to the minute, and he says you're doing a lot."

"I guess I am," I lied.

"Well, if I were you, I'd just stop," she advised. "He'll do a great report, and he'll already have any information you find." I didn't tell her that I already decided I wasn't doing nothin' except the drawing, but I was sure glad to have her approval.

"No, I have to do my part," I said, trying to sound sincere.

"Why don't you come over to our apartment and work on it with Jackson?" she suggested, then smiled. "He'd really like that. A lot."

"When?" I asked.

"Not tonight, because you're not on the schedule – uh, I mean – never mind. Can you come over tomorrow?"

"Maybe. You got a pen and paper? I'll copy down my telephone number for you." She did, so we exchanged numbers. Then I just wanted to get out of there before she caught me in any more lies. I'd already told too many. The one about not following her on the sidewalk, the one about my dad, and the one about working on the report. I had to leave before I told any more lies.

"I gotta go in now," I said. "I'll call you." I walked to my apartment to get showered and changed for the big night with my mom. But I wasn't thinking about that.

I was thinkin' how I could get on Jackson's computer to make him think I was doin' my share of the report. I'd have to find his report, mess it up a little, print it, and bring it to Jackson on Monday. It was a perfect way to trick him. I even had his sister's approval, in a way. She said I shouldn't bother doing the report.

I knew my plan was wrong, but didn't care much. Everyone knows I ain't that good. It's easy to be bad when people expect it from you.

I hoped my mom would let me go over his apartment tomorrow. She prob'ly would.

Chapter Fourteen

The Plan

It was Saturday morning. Mom told me to mind my manners and be back by one to go see Grandma. Then she kissed me on the cheek.

I was sort of excited, so on the way over to Jackson's, I laid my red folder on the sidewalk to do my new trick. I ran as fast as I could across the grass, took a giant skip, did a round-off and then a backflip. I wanted to say "Tuh-Duh!," but there wasn't no one around to say it to. So I trotted back over to my red folder stuffed with blank paper and headed off to Jackson's apartment. By now I figured out that him and his family was rich – they was building a brand-new house. Only rich people can do that, and I wondered how their apartment looked.

Knock, knock.

Jackson's mother opened the door. She was friendly.

"Hello. You must be Hillary. It's so nice to meet you," she greeted me. I remembered what I said about Jackson the first time I saw him: "I ain't workin' with no monkey man," or something like that. I know she heard me. Maybe she forgot. Hopefully.

I smiled and said hello, and she guided me back to the room where Jackson was. He was sitting at a computer.

"It's ten fifty-nine. You're one minute early, but that's okay," he announced with his eyes on his watch. Then he turned back to his computer screen.

I looked around the room, which was totally bombarded with weather information. Wall-to-wall posters of weather charts, weather posters, earth rotation pictures, wind charts, cloud charts, maps, maps, and more maps. All that, and three computers in one room.

"Wow, you've got a lot of stuff here," I said looking around.

"I'm not allowed to talk about the weather posters now. We have to work on our potto report for forty-five minutes. But I can tell you about them later during choice time. That's eleven forty-five, but I have to start my video at twelve."

"That's okay," I said, "I ain't all that interested in weather." Then I grabbed a chair from the other computer table in the room.

"That's my dad's chair, but you can use it," Jackson commented.

"Good," I said. What did he expect me to do? Stand? I got settled in the chair, opened my red folder and spoke again.

"Look, I got my potto stuff here." Then I watched him, until I knew he saw the blank paper. I gasped with fake shock. "Oh no! I brought over the wrong folder. I can't believe I did that." He bought the whole story – hook, line, and sinker.

"Do you want to go home and get it?" he asked.

"No, that's okay. Let's look at what you done, and if I got more, I'll go get it," I answered. He agreed, and then he showed me his work. It was four pages on the computer.

"Wow, that's a lot!" I commented – and it was. I was impressed.

"I divided it up into physical characteristics, diet, habitat, predators, and territorial behavior. I also have some maps and charts ready to print. But it's in another place on the computer. We definitely need to talk about the three subspecies ..."

"Uh, stop for a minute," I sorta yelled to make him stop before he got too detailed, but it didn't work.

"The potto potto, the potto edwardsi, and the potto ibeanus are the three subspecies, but there are two other species that have potto in their names ..." He went on for a while. It was like I hadn't said nothin' to him about being quiet. So I let him blab while I made plans in my head.

I had to figure out some things. First was how to get to his report on the computer, second was how I could get his computer to print, and third was how I could get on his computer without no one in the room. My plan was good – find his report, delete some stuff, change around some words, and then print it. I wouldn't save my changes so it would go back to his old report, and he wouldn't know nothin' about what I done. Monday I could bring him what I copied. He would think I did my fair share. I nodded my head and smiled. It was a good plan. Now it was time to listen to Jackson again.

Boy, could he talk! How much could one person know about pottos? His sister was right – he was like Einstein. I finally got bored.

"Stop!" I yelled louder than before, and then I heard his mom.

"Jackson, are you lecturing?" she asked. She was standing in the doorway with a little red card. I looked at Jackson with his crinkled-up eyebrows.

"I don't think so."

"Yes, you are," she corrected. "No lectures. I've fixed a little snack for you and Hillary. Why don't you come and get it? You and Hillary are allowed to eat in the computer room today."

"No thank you," he replied.

"I didn't ask you a question," his mother said. "I was just telling you what to do in a nice way."

"Oh," he said and then left with his mother to get the snack. It was a perfect time for Part One of my plan. I hit the X in the corner of the screen a couple of times 'til I got to the home page on the computer.

"Sorry, Jackson," I said as he entered the room with a plateful of sliced apples and pears, and some dip for them. "I lost the potto report on your computer. Yours don't work like mine." He looked mad.

"Sorry!" I said again. He huffed and put the plate down.

"There are ten apple slices and ten pear slices. We can have five of each," he said.

"Okay," I replied. "Sorry about the report. I should get it back up on the screen, since I lost it. Can you tell me how?" So he did. He didn't like what I done, losin' his report, and told me about it. But at least I learned how to get to it on the computer.

Part One of my plan – complete.

We spent the next half hour eatin' the snack and workin' on the potto report. By workin' I mean Jackson lectured and I fake listened. Then at eleven forty-five, Jackson announced that it was choice time.

"Now I can tell you about all these maps." He was smiling, like he was all excited or something.

"No," I said and crossed my arms across my chest, just to show him I meant NO. He should've already known I didn't want to hear about them. I told him before.

"It's my choice time so I get to choose," he answered.

"No!" I said again, but then thought about my plan, changed my mind, and made a deal with him: If he showed me how to print out his report, I'd listen while he told me about the maps. He didn't even ask me why I wanted to learn how to print, so I didn't have to give him a reason. Good. One less lie.

Part Two of my plan, learning how to print on his computer – complete.

Actually, it wasn't too bad listening to him blab about his maps. I even learned a new cool word to say: "anemometer." An-uh-MOM-mih-ter. It's hard to say fast three times in a row. But fun to try. If you want to know what it means, ask Jackson. I already forgot.

The third part of my plan would have to happen during his weather video, which started at twelve o'clock sharp. I wasn't sure how I was gonna do it, but as it turned out, Jackson's mom helped me. Actually, I think she felt sorry for me, having to watch his video.

It was awful. Scientists, weathermen, maps, charts, numbers, wind speeds, weather patterns – BORING STUFF, with capital letters. Super-boring. I put my head back on the arm of the couch and admired the huge TV.

Then I turned to look at Jackson. He was sitting on his knees right in front of the gigantic screen. His eyes was staring intently at the TV, and his lips was moving with the speaker on the video. I listened carefully and could hear him saying the words real soft. He had the whole thing memorized, I think.

About that time, Jackson's mom must've noticed me. She called me into the kitchen and told me if I wasn't interested in his video, I could go home. She was real nice about it. I thanked her, but told her I needed to get on the computer to look up some stuff for our report. She told me to go ahead.

So that's when I did the third part of my plan. I got to Jackson's potto report on the computer, deleted some information, changed some words, and royally messed it up. Then I printed out the messed-up report. I didn't save it, and checked it out on the computer. Yep. It went back to Jackson's old, good report. Perfect!

Part Three of my plan – complete.

I stuffed the copy I made in my red folder, said bye to Jackson's mom and left. Jackson never even noticed. He was busy saying all the words to the movie and pointing at charts and numbers and stuff, just like the people on the video was doing.

Slowly I headed home with my red folder. I ain't never been in a home quite like theirs. It was interesting. I tried to say AN- NE- MO- ME- TER three times in a row. But it didn't seem as much fun as before.

Actually, even though I liked Jackson's place, I was feeling kind of bad. I don't know why, 'cause I'd carried off my plan perfect.

Chapter Fifteen

Hotheads and Pencil Geeks

Marnie is another friend in Pamela's group. She's mean, too.

They was all standin' at the pencil sharpener with Jackson. Marnie was first. Pamela was next, then Jackson, then Claudia and Evy. I was watching them instead of doing my morning work. It was Monday morning. Something was up, and I wanted to know what.

They had lots of pencils in their hands. Jackson looked worried. He was staring at his pencils, then glancing at the clock, then back to his pencils. He had a big frown. The girls was lookin' at each other with smiles.

Marnie finally got done, and Pamela waved Claudia past Jackson and ahead of her. He didn't like that. At least, that's how he looked. He bent his elbows and clenched his pencils tightly in front of his chest. Pamela said something to him and turned away. He shook his head back and forth with a real serious look on his face.

Then it happened again. Pamela waved Evy past Jackson and ahead of her. He looked like he was growing even madder. And Pamela – well, she looked happier.

That's when Mrs. Price walked in. She had been in the hall talkin' to another teacher.

"Class, it's eight twenty. You've had plenty of time to sharpen your pencils."

"I've been waiting in line," Pamela said in her sweetest voice. Her fake sweet voice. It made me sick.

"Well, you don't need to sharpen all those. Just one for now. We've got to get to work."

"Okay," Pamela said. "I'll let Jackson go first. He's got all his pencils, you know." It was his habit. In less than a week, everyone knew his pencil problem.

"Jackson, same rule for you," Mrs. Price announced. "Only one for right now." He didn't look like he was payin' no attention to her. He stepped ahead of Pamela, stuck a pencil in the sharpener and cranked it around for a good while. Then he started on the second one.

"Excuse me, Mrs. Price," Pamela interrupted with her hand up in the air. "Didn't you say Jackson could only do one pencil?" Mrs. Price looked at Jackson and spoke to him.

"You need to stop, Jackson. Only one for now." But he was staring at his pencil and cranking the handle.

"Jackson," the teacher said in a louder voice, "stop." But he kept going. Mrs. Price walked over to him. She reached for the extra pencils he had stuffed into his jeans pocket, and he jumped. I mean, he JUMPED!

"Those are my pencils," he said. He stopped the sharpener, grabbed his pencils, and held them all against his chest.

"You only have time to sharpen one now," Mrs. Price repeated.

"But I have to sharpen five," he said.

"Not now," Mrs. Price told him. "You can finish later." He squinted his eyes, frowned, and shook his head.

"Go on, head back to your desk," she said, and then she told Pamela to hurry with her pencil.

So Jackson headed back to his desk and lined up his pencils. It took him a long time. Meanwhile, Mrs. Price explained our schedule change. There was an assembly that afternoon. That meant we wouldn't have no time to work on our science projects after lunch. So we was gonna to work on the projects first. All the morning subjects was gonna be cut short a little. That seemed easy enough to understand.

"Okay, class, let's get together with our partners," Mrs. Price announced. I looked over at Jackson and saw he was still messin' with his pencils. Everyone sat still at first and didn't move.

"Come on, we need to get started," urged Mrs. Price. That's when Jackson reached in his desk and pulled out his reading book. Meanwhile, everyone else was movin' around tryin' to get together with their partners.

I went over to him. "Jackson, we ain't s'posed to be readin' now. Mrs. Price just said."

"We have reading first thing in the morning. That's the schedule," he replied.

"Not today. Wasn't you listenin'? We got a schedule change." I shrugged my shoulders. "That's just the way it is. Ain't no big deal."

Jackson sighed real loud and shook his head. "I don't like it. I don't like today," he griped under his breath.

"Hey, I don't like today either," I agreed. "I don't like no day at school. They all stink."

Jackson sniffed. "Today doesn't stink," he said. "I just don't like today. Not so far."

"Look," I said. "This'll make you like it better." I pulled out the report from my red folder. It was the one I had copied from his computer. The one I'd messed up on purpose. "See, I remembered my report."

He took it from me and studied it. Then he shook his head.

"How long did you spend on this?" he asked.

"How long did you spend on yours?" I asked back. I knew what to do. Whatever he said, I would say a little more.

"Well, not too much time. Twenty-one minutes, not counting my time with you this weekend."

"Yeah, I didn't have much time either. Just twenty-three minutes," I said.

"Your report has lots of mistakes in it." He was real serious.

"Yeah, well you know a lot more about pottos than I do. It's my first time to study them." It was only a half lie. He did know more about it than me, but I didn't do no studyin'. I was congratulating myself on only telling a half lie instead of a whole one when it happened.

Pamela brushed by Jackson's desk and knocked all his pencils to the floor. "Oh, I'm so sorry," she said.

I could tell there wasn't no way she was sorry. She planned it. Jackson told her that was okay and then started frantically picking up his pencils. He didn't like the ones that wasn't sharpened. He kept lookin' at the tips, touching them, and then shaking his head.

Pamela and Evy and Claudia and Marnie was cracking up. I saw them. I glared at them. They was so mean sometimes.

"Here, let me help you," I said to Jackson.

"Look," Pamela whispered. She thought I couldn't hear. "It's Hothead helping Pencil Geek. Pitiful." I was gonna lose my temper. My body got real hard, and my face was turnin' red. I could feel it coming.

"Mrs. Price." Paul spoke loud enough to get her attention. He was a few feet away. I saw him do something to his pencil, but I didn't know what. She stood up and turned around.

"Did someone call my name?" she asked.

"It was me," Paul answered. He held up his pencil with a broken tip. "I've got a pencil problem." Then he glanced at me, who was so angry I thought I was gonna bust, and Jackson, who was touching his pencil tips.

"Paul, you know my rule," Mrs. Price said. "You're supposed to have two sharp pencils ready before class starts."

"Well, I never got up to the sharpener. It was too crowded," Paul answered, and jerked his head toward Pamela and Marnie and the rest of them.

"Go ahead," Mrs. Price said, "you can sharpen that one."

"How about if I do two?" he asked. Then he glanced at me and Jackson again. I think on purpose.

"Why two?" she asked.

"I don't know. I thought you said we're all supposed to have two ready. Just want to follow the rules," he answered. He looked at us a third time, and it was way bigger than a passing glance.

"'Cause he's a pencil geek, too," Pamela whispered. Her and her friends was givin' each other the eyes. But they knew how not to get caught, so they tried not to laugh too much or nothin' like that.

"Okay, go ahead and do two," Mrs. Price said. She headed back to her desk, turned around, and watched all of us. Me and Jackson was gathering his pencils and everyone else was working. After a minute, she came over to Jackson's desk, leaned over and spoke softly.

"Jackson, after Paul's done, would you like to sharpen the rest of your pencils?" Jackson smiled real big.

That's when it dawned on me. Paul was one smart boy. Somehow, he let Mrs. Price know what was goin' on. He knew how to handle them mean girls, Pamela and her friends. And they didn't even know what he done. Ain't that amazing?

Meanwhile, what had I done? I copied Jackson's report, made him think I done it, and acted like I was workin' hard on our report.

I wasn't no better than the other girls in my class. That made me feel bad.

Real, real bad.

Chapter Sixteen

More to the Story

I stopped at the doorway of Jackson's apartment and clenched my fist to knock, but couldn't do it.

I still had to work up my nerve. What was I gonna say? Today was the worst Monday in my entire life. I kinda knew what I should do, but it was gonna be hard. The door opened before I knocked. Jackson's mom stood there, looking down at me.

"Hello, Hillary," she said. She sounded friendly. Maybe she hadn't heard what had happened at school.

"Hello."

"Would you like to come in?"

"Sure." I stepped inside the door.

"Jackson," she called, "Hillary's here."

"I still have one more minute. It's on the schedule," Jackson yelled back. He sounded like he was in the computer room.

"Would you like something to drink?" Mrs. Thomas asked.

"No thanks." I knew she knew what had happened. Otherwise, she would've sent me back to the computer room. We was gonna talk, and she was settin' me up for it. I sat down on the big soft chair in the living room and waited. She went back to get Jackson.

"I'm sorry," I blurted out as soon as they returned. "I really didn't mean to hurt you, Jackson. You was just in the way, and I threw the stupid thing wrong." The stupid thing was actually this soft, squishy ball that Mrs. Lorrey gave me. Sometimes, when I get real mad, I squeeze it. It helps me settle down. That's all I'm supposed to use it for. Nothing else.

Not throwing, like what I done.

"I'm glad you came over," said Mrs. Thomas. She had called me as soon as I got home from school and asked me over. I told my mom where I was going when she called, but didn't tell her what happened at school. I didn't tell her I was kicked out of school and got a ride back to our apartment with Mrs. Lorrey. I didn't tell her I was planning on being sick for two days. I didn't tell her they don't have her phone numbers right at school 'cause I changed them on the enrollment form. That was a long time ago when I was still so mad at her.

"Discussion time is thirty minutes," Jackson said. "Then the

Weather Channel comes on." His eye was red and bruised and swollen from where I hit him.

"Jackson, did you hear what Hillary said?" his mom asked.

"She said sorry."

"I'm kicked out of school for two days, so I can't go to the library with you. I'll just fix up the potto picture, I guess. Would that be all right with you?" I asked him.

"Yes, that's all right," he agreed. Then his mom spoke.

"Hillary, I need to thank your mom for letting you come over."

"I'll tell her," I said. A lie to cover up a lie.

"Thanks," she answered, and then got to what she really wanted to say. "I know you've been suspended, but I think there's more to the story. I've heard that from people at school. That's why I asked you to come over." I was really surprised. She heard it from people at school? I wondered who. And what they said.

"I want to tell the story first. Is that okay?" asked Jackson, like he was gonna tell a fun little event or something. So he did. It was so wrong! And so short. He left out every important part there was.

"Hillary threw her ball at me and hit me in the eye, and it might turn black and blue," he said. I waited for more, but nothing came.

"That's it?" I asked. "That's the whole story?"

"Well," he thought and thought, and finally said, "You told me my friends were mean." I looked at Jackson's mom and shook my head.

"Okay, Jackson. Now it's Hillary's turn. This is a discussion, so it's your turn to listen," she said.

"Well, here's the story," I began. And I told it in a lot of detail. It was way different than his.

First of all, I told about Pamela and Evy and Claudia and Marnie, and the pencil sharpener and the pencils. Then I told what happened with them on the playground. At recess, they went up to Jackson and started copying him.

They spun around in circles and did the finger movements and all the weird stuff he does sometimes. He laughed and did it more. They was pointing at him and laughing at him and making fun of him. Me and Jenny was watchin' and talkin' about it. We knew what they was doing, 'cause they done it to us before.

"No, that's not right. We were making jokes together," Jackson interrupted.

"You need to listen," his mom said. She looked at me and I looked at her and said, "I'm not tryin' to be mean or nothin' like that, but they was making fun of him."

"No they weren't!" Jackson insisted.

"It ain't just you," I said. "They make fun of me and Jenny and all the kids that ain't in their group. They're mean."

Jackson breathed real hard and looked angry. I started in again. He tried to look at his squiggling fingers, but his mom wouldn't let him. She told him to pay attention.

"Then Jackson comes over to me and Jenny and asks if it's okay to call Jenny healthy. You know about how big Jenny is, don't you?" I asked Mrs. Thomas. She did, so I continued.

"Well, Jenny's feelings got hurt, and I asked Jackson why he said that." Then I turned to him and said, "So tell your mom why. Go ahead, tell her just what you told me."

"Because they said that healthy is a nice word to use. They said Jenny liked to be called healthy and that was a good name for her. They told me to ask her. They said you were wrong about healthy. It's a real nice compliment in our school."

"That's what they said to you?" his mom asked.

"Yeah, because they are really nice. They laugh at my jokes and we're friends."

"No, Jackson," his mother said, "Hillary is right. They are not your friends." He crinkled his eyebrows.

"Friends don't hurt other people's feelings," his mom continued.

"They didn't hurt my feelings," Jackson argued.

"But they tried to get you to hurt Jenny's feelings, and you did. You hurt her feelings again, Jackson," his mom said.

"Jenny's not my friend, and healthy is a good word. That's what my friends told me," he insisted. That made me mad!

"You've GOT to be kidding! Jenny is the nicest person in the whole class behind your back. She IS your friend. She sticks up for you! Pamela and them mock you and me and everyone else they don't like." I folded my arms across my chest and glared at him.

"They do, too, like me," Jackson insisted. I shook my head and looked at his mom. She shrugged her shoulders and put out her hands.

"Go on with the rest of your story," she said.

"Well, I got a real bad temper problem," I explained.

"So you lost your temper?"

"Yeah, when I found out what Pamela and them girls done, I guess I just exploded." I paused, then added, "I think I scared Jackson, 'cause he ran back to them stupid girls."

"But how did you hit him?" she asked.

"Well, I ran over and threw this squishy ball real hard at Pamela. I wanted to knock her mouth off her face. But I missed and it flew right past her into Jackson's eye." Mrs. Thomas shook her head.

"Geez, you shouldn't have done that," she said.

"I know." I hung my head.

"But now the story makes sense," she added. "Now I get it." It was my turn to talk. I lifted my head.

"I'm sorry that I hit you, Jackson. And I'm sorry if I scared you when I got mad. But them girls used you. They used you to hurt Jenny." He shook his head no.

Anyways, that's all his mom wanted to hear. I didn't tell her what happened after that. I was yanked off the playground and got an automatic suspension for what I done. Didn't matter why. I shouldn't be throwin' nothing at people. They couldn't get a hold of my mom, and they didn't want me on the bus, so Mrs. Lorrey drove me home. I didn't talk to no one that afternoon, not even Mrs. Lorrey. I was so upset. Really upset.

"Hillary," Mrs. Thomas said when I was getting ready to leave, "thanks for coming over and explaining."

"You're welcome," I said. I was glad she gave me the chance and wanted her to know I didn't really blame Jackson. "It ain't Jackson's fault what he done, is it? There's something wrong with him, ain't there?"

"There might be," Mrs. Thomas said bending down towards me, "but it's important to remember this: There's something a little wrong with all of us, don't you think?"

I smiled and nodded. Ain't that the truth!

Chapter Seventeen

Seeing the Good

WHAM! The door slammed shut.

"Hillary Kate Branson!" I sat up in my bed, stared straight ahead, and swallowed hard. This was trouble. Big trouble. Mom had left fifteen or twenty minutes ago to go see Grandma. Now she was back, and there she stood in my doorway.

"Do you know Mrs. Thomas?" she asked. Oh no, I thought,

she musta met Jackson's mom. There was anger oozing out from every word she said. "It's a good thing we look alike, or she might not have asked me if I was your mom." I really did look a lot like my mom. That's what everyone said.

"Yes, m'am." I said. I never messed with her when she was mad.

"Well, can you guess what she told me?" I shook my head no. I wasn't gonna do no guessin'. That would make her even more mad.

"Well, let's go through the list. Number one: You're suspended from school, so I'm guessing you ain't sick today. You just faked it. Right?" She paused. "And you better not lie." I nodded.

"Number two: You gave her son, I think his name is Jackson, a black eye at school yesterday. Is that true?" I nodded again.

"Number three: You been workin' hard on your computer here every evening? What computer? We ain't even got a working TV, let alone a computer!" I just looked at her. My stomach was full of butterflies.

"I'm calling the school right now. I can't believe they didn't contact me about this. That just ain't right. What's wrong with them?"

"I changed the telephone numbers on the enrollment form," I muttered. I knew I had to tell her before she found out what I done. If I didn't, it would be bad. It was bad now, but it could be worse.

To make a long story short, I was grounded to my room, and Mom was headin' over to the school. But what I was most worried about wasn't being in trouble. It was about her turning bad again, like before. I was gonna drive Mom to her old ways. She started crying, 'cause she's working so hard and trying to be responsible to me and Grandma and her work. And she thinks I'm falling apart. She thinks I don't talk to her no more and don't tell the truth and am mad all the time. Then I cried, 'cause I AM bad, even when I try not to be. What if she turned to her old ways again, all because of me?

I sat on my bed and curled my knees to my chest. Alone in our apartment. Mom was gone to my school, and I was scared. I didn't know what was gonna happen. I rocked and daydreamed. About Jackson, of all people. Somehow, it helped me, thinking about him.

If I could be like Jackson, I could have a mom that didn't have to work. And I could have lots of nice things, like three computers and a big-screen TV. And I could have a sister who I would talk to. But almost anyone could have those things.

Except me.

There was something else about Jackson that was different than other people, something that was special. And good. I was tryin' to put my finger on it. It was hard, but I was figuring it out.

For one thing, he don't lie. He don't even know when people are lyin' to him. That's why he believed Pamela and her friends. That's why he thinks I'm doing my fair share. I think he don't even know how to lie. He'd be really bad at it if he tried. I sure could teach him.

I wish I could take a pill to make me as honest as he is. Just for one day, to see what it was like. If I could, maybe I would find out what it would be like to just say who I am and not be embarrassed. Jackson can do that. He tells everyone what he wants them to know and don't worry what they think. Like yesterday – a perfect example.

It was late morning, and the pre-K busses was there to take the morning kids home.

"Mrs. Price," the principal called over the intercom, "could you send Jackson to the office, please."

"Sure. Go on, Jackson," she said.

"Is it my practice time?" he asked.

"Yeah, that's probably what it is," she answered.

"I get to practice sitting in the third row of the bus. I did it with chairs in Mrs. Lorrey's room. It was easy," Jackson said loud enough for the whole class to hear. Some kids giggled, but he didn't seem to care. "It's hard changing bus seats, you know," he added.

"Just go on, Jackson," said Mrs. Price. So he left. Forty-five minutes later he came back.

"I did it," he announced proudly when he walked in the room. "I rode the third-row seat of the bus all the way around the bus route." He was beaming, like he had just done something great. "Next year, I'm going to ride in other seats, too. I'm going to practice this summer."

"So you rode the bus route with the pre-K kids?" one of the boys asked. "Just to practice sitting in the third row?"

"Yeah, it was easy," Jackson said again.

"Class," Mrs. Price said in a slightly threatening voice, "get busy on your work." She said it like that to stop the laughing. At least, that's what I thought. But she couldn't stop the looks. Almost everyone stared at Jackson. Some traded looks and rolled their eyes.

"It should have been embarrassing," I said to no one while I rocked back and forth on my bed. "How did he stop hisself from being embarrassed?" I wanted to learn how to do that.

And there was some other stuff he needed to teach me, too. Like how to turn things inside out and backwards. He does that good. What someone says don't matter a lot of times, 'cause he turns it on its head. That's what he done when we came in from recess last week.

We was lining up on the edge of the playground, and Jackson was gonna be last in line. He stayed out in the middle of the field spinning instead of coming in when the whistle blew. He should have got in trouble for makin' us all wait. Me and Jenny knew he liked to be last, and so did the teacher, I think.

When he finally got in to where we all was all standing, Mrs. Price said, "I hope you don't think you're being slick, pretending like you didn't hear me, just so you can be last. That's how you get in trouble in this class." She thought for a moment and added, "Now come up here to the front of the line." But he didn't. He stayed right there and got a real serious look on his face.

"I thought slick meant slippery," he said, and slid his hand up and down his arm. "I'm not slick." The teacher shook her head.

"That's not what I meant," she said.

"Unless you put soap on me," he added. "Then I can get real slick." I looked at him like he was nuts and tried to explain in a whisper.

"Uh, she wasn't talkin' about that Jackson. It's just you was slick, like you was clever how you got to come in last."

"Oh," he said real loud, "so slick is an idiom. It means clever, and I was being slick the idiom, not slick the slippery meaning. Is that what you meant?"

Mrs. Price looked at him, grinned a little, and nodded. Just like that, he got outta trouble. He stayed last in line and made the teacher smile. It's funny what he does with words. It's like he makes a joke. It works for him, but he don't even know what he done. He's slick in that way, or maybe there's a better word. Can you be slick and not know it? That's him, but I don't know a word for what he does.

○ ○ ○

My rocking had stopped. I was just sitting on my bed with my chin on my knees and my arms around my legs. I smiled a little because I remembered something else. Something important. For a while Jackson didn't seem to know I was bad. He even bragged to the teacher about me being a good partner. It's kind of nice thinking about that, 'cause I wanna be good. It's just hard sometimes, 'specially when no one thinks I can do it.

I rolled over on my side and dozed off.

The clicking of the lock woke me up. My mom had returned from the school. I lay there and wondered what she was going to say.

"Hill," she said by the door to my room. I rolled over and looked at her. "I'm calling my work and telling them I can't come in today."

"Okay." I wondered why. I hoped she wasn't quitting her job 'cause of me.

"Right now, I have to go see Grandma for a little bit. It's important," she said and then added, "Would you like to come?" I shook my head no. I didn't want no one askin' me why I wasn't in school.

"You have to be punished for what you done, but you know I love you, don't you?" She walked over to me, leaned over, and kissed my cheek. "And in case you don't know, you're a good kid. Real good."

Jackson and Mom, two people in the world that could actually see the good in me, at least for a little while.

Maybe I could work with that.

Chapter Eighteen

Ann Drew Jackson

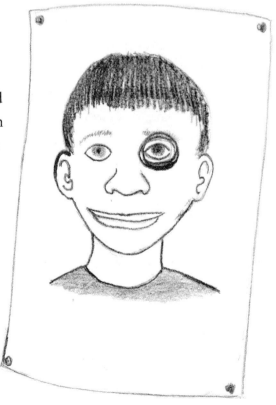

Finally, I got back to school. Mom took two days off work and stayed at home with me. I had to clean every stupid thing in the house and stay in my room and do school work. Oh, and I had to listen to her talk. She tried to get me to open up, as she put it. I guess that was nice, but I got tired of it. I don't like opening up that much.

It felt good to be in school again, but it was

too bad that I had to wait until Thursday. We have art two times a month on Wednesdays, and I missed it. That stunk.

We was in the hallway waiting to use the bathroom. Mrs. Price sent in five kids at a time, so it took a while. While we was waiting, she allowed us to look at the pictures on the wall, the ones that everyone drew in art class.

"What did you do in art yesterday?" I asked Jenny.

"We had to draw portraits," she said, and then she explained in more detail. "Everybody chose a partner and we had to try to draw each other. Actually, just our faces, thank heavens. I wouldn't want anyone drawing my body." Sometimes she made fun of herself like that, but only to me – no one else. It was her way of joking. I shook my head at her and smiled.

"So who was your partner?" I asked.

"Tasha. I had to kind of fix it up a little after she was done. We were allowed to do that." She stopped talking and we looked at the pictures. I was trying to figure out who was who.

Bump. I was concentrating real hard and accident'ly stepped sideways right into Ann, this girl in our class. I don't know her that good. She don't say much, but she's pretty good at drawing.

"Oops, sorry."

"That's okay," she answered.

And that's when I spotted it. It was a picture of Jackson, black eye and all. Actually, it was very good, except for the black eye part – an ugly circle scribbled around his eye. It looked like them dogs that have a black ring around one of their eyes. I seen Jackson today. I'd been watchin' him all morning, wondering if he was still mad at me. He did have a bruise under his eye, but it wasn't that bad.

"I wonder who drew Jackson," I said, kind of to myself.

"I did," said Ann.

"You did? How did you end up with him as a partner?"

"We were the last two left," she said. I could see that. She's so quiet, and he ain't the kind of person anyone would pick for a partner.

"It's a good picture, except for the black eye," I said. To me, she was making a big deal out of what I done, givin' Jackson the black eye. It made me a little mad.

"I didn't make that part. Jackson added it after I was finished," she said.

"Oh." What else was I s'pose to say?

"Yeah, he said it had to be there because the teacher said to be exact."

"Did you tell him he ain't gonna have a black eye in a week or so?" I asked. "That it's gonna go away and then it won't be exact no more?"

"Yeah, but he didn't care. He said since he had a black eye, it had to be there. That was exact. I even asked the teacher."

"What did she say?"

"She said it didn't have to be there. But Jackson said he had a black eye and that's exactly what he looks like." She shrugged her shoulders.

I could see Jackson doing that, but it hurt my feelings. It was like a reminder of what I done. I wish Pamela had the black eye. I wouldn't mind looking at that.

It was a couple of hours later at lunch when this portrait thing made Jackson do what he does best: He turned the whole lunchroom conversation inside out and backwards. I figured out the way he does this inside-out-backwards thing. He just catches the little bits and turns the whole conversation on its head.

Some of us was sitting at lunch talking about the portraits. I was at the end of the group until the lunch lady, Mrs. White, took up for Jackson. He was getting ready to sit by hisself.

"Hey, over here, Jackson," she called to him. "You can sit with the rest of the kids." So he moved over beside me like he wasn't even mad at me or nothing. That was good. Then he took out his tornado snacks from his lunch sack and started counting them.

"Okay," says Jenny to everyone, "you know those portraits? Well, Hillary wasn't even here yesterday, and she can name who drew who. Almost everybody, I think."

"How many do you know?" asked Tasha.

"Hmmm," I said, and thought about which ones I knew. "I know a lot, 'cause I asked around. But not everybody."

"Then do it. Let's check it out," says Michael from the other end of our group. He was kind of between the boys and the girls, but was listening in on us girls.

"Just name them," he said, "and I'll count the ones that are right." So I started. I got through a bunch of them when I remembered a couple of easy ones.

"Oh yeah, Jenny drew Tasha, and Tasha drew Jenny," I said. They nodded.

"And Jackson drew Ann," I said, turning a little towards Jackson so he could hear me. He was almost finished arranging his tornado snacks in groups.

"And Ann drew Jackson. That's all I know." I smiled. I was proud.

"That's the president," Jackson said, more to his snacks than to any of us. Maybe I didn't hear him right. It didn't make no sense.

"What did you say?" asked Jenny.

"That's the president," he said louder, so everyone could hear.

"Oh," me and Jenny said together. We looked at each other.

"What are you talking about?" asked Michael, "I think I missed something." He was leaning towards us, trying to listen.

"Well, he's the seventh president. He was the first president born in a log cabin. Abraham Lincoln was born in a log cabin, too, but he wasn't first," Jackson answered loudly.

"Which president?" Michael and Tasha asked in unison. Everybody, and I mean everybody, was looking at Jackson. I think that's what we was all wondering.

"Andrew Jackson," he answered.

"Why you talking about Andrew Jackson?" I asked.

"You said his name first. I was trying to stay on the subject," he insisted.

"Oh, well, I don't think we was really talking about him," I said. I was trying to be nice, because of his black eye. Every time I looked at it, I felt bad.

"I heard you say Andrew Jackson," he said. I shook my head no, but didn't say nothing. I was confused. Michael was the one that finally figured it out.

"Jackson," he called across the table with a big smile, "Hillary didn't say Andrew Jackson, the president. She said Ann." He stopped and pointed to Ann. She was sitting across from him, but was quiet as usual.

"Drew," and he pretended like he was drawing in the air, "your portrait yesterday," and he kind of put a frame around his head with his arms. Jackson sat there a few seconds and thought about what Michael said. Then I could tell it dawned on him what had happened. His whole face lit up.

"Ooooohhhh," he said stretching it out real long. "I get it now. It's not Andrew, one word, it's Ann and then drew, two words." Very slowly, word by word, he put it together: "Ann – drew – Jackson." He started to laugh. We all did. It was good, 'cause we was laughing with him, not at him. Mrs. White came over and told us to hush up, so we quieted down.

"Was that an idiom?" Jackson asked me after a few minutes.

"What?" I asked back.

"Ann drew Jackson," he said real slow.

"I don't know. I don't think so." But I'll tell you what it was. Funny. Just plain funny. The best joke I've heard in a long time." He smiled and I smiled.

Suddenly, I was feeling more confident. I knew what I had to do.

For two solid days while I was home I had been thinking about the conversation I needed to have. It was gonna be hard for me. Real hard. But I could do it.

That's 'cause me and Jackson was smilin' together. He wasn't mad no more.

Chapter Nineteen

The Whole Truth and Nothing But the Truth

"So let's see what you have here," said Mrs. Price. She was looking over everyone's science projects, and it was our turn. Tomorrow was the big presentation day, and she was making sure we was ready.

Jackson pulled out everything he had typed. Plus all these pictures of pottos in the jungle. And maps of where they lived. There was even pictures of potto skeletons and organs. It was ridiculous how much stuff he had.

All I had was the pictures I drew. They was prob'ly the best ones I ever done in my whole life. One was for the front of the report cover and the other for the back. I made sure I spent five hours drawing. That was the only way I could honestly say I spent the same amount of time on the report as Jackson. It also meant there was a lot of detail. My green and brown pencils was little nubs by the time I was finished. I pulled out my red folder that held the pictures.

"This is really quite a bit. You two have done a fantastic job," Mrs. Price said. She was leafing through all the stuff Jackson had. "Do you have a folder or something to put it in?"

"I have this red folder," I offered. "It ain't that good lookin', but I was gonna cover it up with the pictures I made."

"It ISN'T that good-looking," Mrs. Price corrected me.

"Yeah, it isn't," I repeated. Then I pulled my pictures out of the folder. The teacher and Jackson just stared at them for a little while.

"Wow, Hillary, these are fantastic," Mrs. Price finally said. "Let me figure out a way you can attach them to a folder without glue. I don't want you to ruin them. They are really amazing."

"Okay," I said. It made me feel good, but I knew the hard part was coming up. I never did have the conversation with Jackson, so that meant I had to have it with him AND Mrs. Price. For two days I had been telling myself to do it. I even practiced what I was gonna say in my bedroom. Now was the time.

"So how long did this take you?" Mrs. Price was talking to me, but Jackson answered.

"I spent a total of five hours and seven minutes. We were keeping track of time to make sure Hillary did her fair share. She was ahead of me by seven minutes on Monday, but I added time, so ..."

"Okay, Jackson, that's plenty of time," Mrs. Price interrupted. I swallowed hard. The time for telling the truth had arrived. I started out with the easy part.

"Actually, I spent about five hours, too," I said.

"I did seven minutes more, so that means you didn't do your fair share. I did seven extra minutes," Jackson commented.

"The time you both spent is close enough together that we can say Hillary did her fair share. It's about the same amount. It doesn't have to be exact," said Mrs. Price, and then came the part I did not want to hear. "She did these beautiful pictures and helped out with all this information, too." She picked up the stack of papers Jackson brought in. "You have to admit, that's a lot."

"Yes, it is," he said, in total agreement. The moment had come for me to confess. It was now or never. I was really nervous.

"Umm-well," and that's all that came out. I tried again. "Umm," then I took in a deep breath and started a third time. "Um, I think Jackson's right. I didn't really do my fair share," I finally said.

"Why do you say that?" asked Mrs. Price.

"Um, well, I actually didn't do any of that." I pointed to Jackson's stack of papers.

"Yes you did," said Jackson. "Remember, you came over my house?"

"I know," I said.

"And you brought in the report on Monday and gave it to me." He actually looked at me when he spoke that time – not at my hair.

"Yeah, but ..." I stopped. I had to hold back the tears. There was a big, solid lump in my throat. This was hard. Way harder than I thought it would be. I closed my eyes for a few seconds and got myself back to normal. Sort of, but it took a while for the lump to get small enough to be able to talk. Then I said what I done, every last detail.

The whole truth and nothing but the truth.

1. I tricked Jackson into showing me how to get onto his report on his computer.
2. I tricked him into showing me how to print on his computer.
3. I got into his report, changed the wording and stuff, copied it, didn't save it, and showed the copy to Jackson on Monday.
4. I lied to Jackson about my fair share. Up until the last two days, I didn't spend no time on the science project.
5. I didn't do no work on the writing and looking-up-information side of our report. Zero.
6. Oh yeah, and we didn't have to do pottos, 'cause I made up all that stuff about P.

Mrs. Price listened and shook her head. Jackson listened and crinkled his forehead.

"Sorry," I said with a cracked voice. "I'm real sorry." Then I looked at the floor and waited for the fallout. There was a silence that seemed to last forever. I felt a tissue wiping the tears from my cheek and looked up. It was Jackson.

"Don't cry. You did your fair share. Mrs. Price said so."

He cares about me, I thought. I just didn't expect that from him – it amazed me. The lump in my throat grew smaller, and a little hopeful feeling crept inside of me.

"You're not mad?" I asked.

"Not really, because you shouldn't have done all that stuff," he said, which confused me. Then he added, "But you did spend five hours making the picture and I spent five hours and seven minutes on the report. You can catch up to me tonight if you work seven more minutes. Then it will be fair, not just fair share." And he smiled.

"Jackson, that is very generous of you," said Mrs. Price, "and I'm sure you'll get a wonderful grade on this report. But Hillary and I will discuss her grade in private."

"Will we discuss my grade in private, too?" he asked.

"If you want, but I'm sure it will be fine." He looked towards me and gave me a thumbs-up.

"That means your grade will be fine, too," he whispered, as if Mrs. Price couldn't hear. "Because we're partners and we did our fair share, so we get the same grade." I nodded at him and didn't bother saying what I thought was pretty clear – my grade was gonna have to be way lower, maybe failing, for what I done.

"Jackson, would you mind bringing this note to Mrs. Lorrey?" Mrs. Price asked. I peeked at what she was writing, but could only read one word before she covered it up: Breakthrough.

"It's not my time to see her," he said. "I see her on Tuesday and Friday at one thirty, unless she tells me different. She didn't tell me about today."

"That's okay. This is important." Mrs. Price folded up the note and taped it shut. He took it and left the room.

Uh, oh. I wondered what she was going to say.

"Hillary, did your mom help you with your decision?" she said.

"What decision?" I asked.

"To tell the truth about everything."

"No, she don't even know," I said.

"She doesn't, not don't," Mrs. Price corrected me.

"She doesn't," I repeated.

"Did you tell Mrs. Lorrey about this?" she asked.

"No, she don't, I mean, doesn't know either." We sat quietly for a little while.

"Well, that was brave of you," Mrs. Price commented. "You didn't have to tell the truth. It was a decision you made. A good one." She gently touched my shoulder and asked me a simple question.

"Why did you do it? What made you tell the truth in such a big way?"

"I dunno," I answered. But I really did. I just didn't want to talk about it no more.

I didn't want to be mean like Pamela and all them girls. They was terrible to Jackson, and I didn't want to be nothin' like that.

And I kind of wanted to see what it would be like to be as honest as Jackson. I liked how he told the truth, no matter what. I admired that about him.

But most important – it was the right thing to do. My mom told me for two days that the right thing to do was sometimes the hardest. But then, after you done it, it felt real good. I wasn't sure about that. It sounded like grown-up blather. But I decided to try it, just in case.

So far so good. I did feel a little better.

But I didn't know about my grade yet. Maybe that would make me feel bad again. I'd find out in a minute.

Chapter Twenty

Feeling Fine

The wind blew through my hair. I wanted to swing up to the clouds and shout out as loud as I could. I was feeling better than I ever felt in a long, long time.

Mom talked to her bosses at work. They was gonna let her change shifts. Tomorrow was pay day, so

she could pay off the car. And Monday would be her first day on the early-morning shift. That meant she would get off work early enough to be at home when I got there. Or maybe a little later if she had to spend a lot of time with Grandma. But no more long nights alone. I was so happy!

Oh, and Jackson, he did the funniest thing today. He zinged Pamela, but he didn't really mean to. She got what she deserved, at last.

It was the very end of the day. We was doing our weekly "brain-building activity." This time, we had to tell what something reminded us of and why. And then the next person had to do the same thing to the last person's idea. So here's how it went:

Mrs. Price: "Pool."

Michael: "Pool. Pool reminds me of board because you dive off a diving board at a pool."

Tasha: "Board. Board reminds me of nail because you hammer nails into a board."

Evy: "Nail. Nail reminds me of Pamela because Pamela has beautiful nails." (They was long and painted with glittery pink polish.)

Jackson: (pause for a long time, then a reminder from the teacher that his word was "Pamela;" then a big smile and a pointer finger in the air like he had a great idea) "Pamela reminds me of koala bears because they're both cute, but watch out – they can hurt you real bad with their long sharp claws."

I looked at Pamela. Her mouth was open, and her hand slowly came up to cover her face.

"Jackson, that was not nice," said Mrs. Price.

"It's supposed to be nice because Pamela's nails are very pretty and pink. But they're long and can scratch, which hurts. And a koala has long sharp claws. So that's how they are alike," Jackson explained. It didn't sound right to me. I thought what he said – 'but watch out, they can hurt you real bad with their long sharp claws' – meant they was both mean. I was pretty sure about that. Poor Jackson – he don't even know what he's saying sometimes.

Mrs. Price put her hands on her hips and looked around the class. She stopped when she got to Jenny and kept her eyes right there. I knew why, since Pamela and her was doing koala bears for their project. Mrs. Price kept staring.

"Was this YOUR idea, Jackson? Or somebody else's?" she asked without turning her eyes towards him. She wanted a certain answer – Jenny – that was clear from where she was lookin'. But Jackson didn't give it to her.

"No, it was everybody's idea. They were all saying it and laughing in the cafeteria. Mrs. White had to make us get quiet." Nobody said nothin', but they sure was looking back and forth between each other. There was a few little grins, too. Personally, I had a great big one. Pamela finally got a little of what she deserved.

Later I found out what happened. When I was gone, Pamela and Evy and them had lunch detention for what they done to Jenny. Everyone was talkin' about them and how mean they was. I sure wished I could have been there. I thought everyone liked Pamela except me and Jenny. It was news to find out I was wrong.

I pumped myself in the air and thought about the rest of the things that happened that afternoon – all good.

For one thing, Mrs. Price told me she's gonna put my potto pictures in an art contest. That's how much she loves them.

Oh, and Mrs. Price ain't gonna give me a bad grade. She said I could get one grade below Jackson. Actually, it was gonna be two grades below. That's what she told me. Then Jackson found out.

"Don't be sad," he had said. It was kind of sweet. He musta thought getting two grades below him should upset me. But really I was thankful that Mrs. Price wasn't gonna fail me. What I done was real bad.

Jackson didn't have no idea how I felt and took matters into his own hands. First he raised his hand real high and kept it there a long, long time. It was like he didn't care that Mrs. Price had her back towards us. That's sort of his way. He don't notice stuff like that. Finally she turned, saw Jackson's hand, and came to us.

"That's not right," he told her when she got to us.

"What's not right?" Mrs. Price asked.

"Hillary worked seven minutes shorter than me. You said that was close enough to be considered her fair share. That means we should get the same grade."

"But she doesn't know anything about pottos except how to draw them," she answered. "This is not an art project. It's a science project. She didn't do the most important part, learning about the animal. You did it all. She understands that. Right, Hillary?" I nodded my head. Jackson scrunched his eyebrows and got real serious.

"Do you know anything about pottos?" he asked me.

"Yeah, they're monkeys," I answered. At least I knew that.

"No they're not!" he blurted out, like I said a really dumb thing. "Remember, they're primates, not monkeys. They're actually Prosimians, and belong in the Lorisidae family." Them big words rolled off his tongue like they was real easy to say.

"I didn't know that," I said and shrugged my shoulders.

"I know a way you can make your grade a little higher, say, one grade below Jackson's instead of two," offered Mrs. Price.

"How?" I asked.

"You can take home this report tonight," she stopped and lifted up all the papers Jackson done, then continued, "and prepare the oral report for tomorrow. That way, I'll know you learned something about the potto. What do you think?"

"I have the oral report ready," Jackson said. "I'm going to do it." I was quiet about the whole thing, 'cause I was satisfied with two grades below. They was both thinking I wanted a higher grade.

"How about if you prepare a report, Hillary, and then Jackson adds all the information you leave out," Mrs. Price suggested. BAD idea! Did Mrs. Price have any idea how much stuff Jackson knew about pottos? He could go on forever.

"If Jackson is ready and wants to do it, then I think he should," I said. It was a good way for me to back out. But it didn't work. Jackson was so worried about my grade and Mrs. Price was practically begging me to change my mind, so I did. We was gonna do the report together. Me first, him next, with a limit of ten minutes. The time limit was my idea, knowing how much Jackson knew about pottos and how much he always talked.

I was gonna get one grade below Jackson. That would be a B, I thought, 'cause I knew Jackson would get an A. Not bad! And I pumped harder to get my swing up real high. "Thanks, Jackson," I thought, and I meant it.

And I needed to thank him for my pictures, too. He's the reason they're gonna go in the art contest. If he hadn't done all that timing of "fair share," I wouldn't have never spent five hours on them. That's why they're so good.

And I needed to thank him for tellin' Pamela what she needed to know – that she might look good on the outside, but she ain't really that great. She's mean, and people know it and talk about it and laugh about it. I'm not sure if Jackson knew what he actually done. But it was good what he said about Pamela. Maybe, just maybe, she would learn a little something about being nice.

My feet dragged the ground a little, and a new idea floated into my brain. Of all the people in the world, who would have ever thought Jackson would be the one to help me? But he is. He's the reason I ended up telling the truth. Ain't no doubt about it. And that was a real, real hard thing for me to do.

I slowed down the swing a little more, jumped off, and ran hard to do a backflip. What a great day it was turning out to be!

I was headin' over to Jackson's apartment soon. We was gonna do our oral report together. I wasn't gonna cheat or nothin', and I was plannin' on doing my fair share.

Oh, and tomorrow I was gonna tell Mrs. Lorrey I wanted to be in her group with Jackson. Now I could give some real good reasons why we should be in a group together.

And they would all be true.

Chapter Twenty-One

Jackson, Through and Through

"Hey, Hillary!" Liz shouted. I had just finished working on my report with Jackson and was heading home. Actually, I just had to memorize the first part of his report. He liked it that way and I did, too. That's 'cause I didn't have to write nothin', and he didn't have to change nothin'. We was a good team. He was smart and knew lots of stuff, and I could draw good and memorize fast.

I turned around. Liz was running towards me with something in her hand. "Here, I want you to read this," she said, handing me a piece of paper. "It's about Jackson." I read it.

"Wow," I said, "this is really nice."

"Thanks," she answered, then smiled.

"Who's Tyler Carson?" I asked. His name was at the bottom of the paper.

"A boy back in his old school. His teacher sent it to us. She thought we'd like it."

"He musta been good friends with Jackson," I commented.

"Probably was, but not like you. You're the first friend Jackson ever had that came over to our place to visit."

"Really?" I said. That was sort of sad.

"Yeah, so Mom and I wanted you to see this."

"But why? What did I do?"

"Well, I know you gave him a black eye," she said with a smile, "but in your own very special way, you've really helped him."

"How?" I asked.

"You gave him a chance, and that's what he really needs."

"Thanks," I said, but I was a little confused. I didn't really do nothin' for him. In fact, he was the one that gave me a chance. Ain't that funny? And his sister don't even know it.

I read the paper one more time before I handed it back. It was Jackson through and through. Maybe one day I'll be like him. I'll make a difference to someone so big that they'll write a poem about me.

I hope so.